Folklore Studies

Local and Global

Folklore Studies
Local and Global

Edited by

M. Mani Meitei
R.K. Dhawan

Prestige Books International
New Delhi

Published by
Prestige Books International
New Delhi 110 060
prestigebooks@gmail.com
Phone: 9818755529

Associate Office
11B, Broomwood Road
London SW11 6HU

Associate Office
P.O. Box 2250
Sydney 2001

ISBN: 978-81-943009-2-2

Printed in India

Contents

Folklore Studies: Local and Global Introduction

M. MANI MEITEI and R.K. DHAWAN

Folklore is the earliest manifestation of human civilization in verbal and expressive form of art. To know folklore is to know our cultural heritage, and through it each one of us gains and acquires knowledge and information and amusement. Folklore constitutes living traditions which have been handed down from generation to generation, and no one is able to specify the exact dates of the origins of various genres of folklore with any degree of accuracy. Characteristically it remains anonymous. Layers and layers of folkloric items exist in human society as cultural treasures but meaningful investigation into these diverse aspects of human mind that created such inexhaustible wealth of human civilization is of paramount importance for the present generation of scholars. Over the years, folklore has grown into becoming an academic discipline especially in the West, Europe and America, and that genuine research and research findings of pioneering scholars have laid models for the study of and research in folklore in the present world is not an exaggeration.

In many parts of the world other than Europe and America, folklore is still a misunderstood subject as if it had challenged and claimed the status of other disciplines in universities and institutions. This attitude has dampened the growth and development of folklore studies in countries like India, and for want of academic and administrative zeal, the discipline has remained eclipsed and continued to remain an academic field of secondary importance. But its importance cannot be overlooked for that reason. Folklore has become an engrossing and engaging discipline, an area of investigation and research calling for the attention of scholars, academics and researchers to broaden its academic and intellectual sphere which would challenge the earlier assumptions and misconceptions about the subject. In order to validate and legitimize this field of enquiry as an independent discipline, ethnologists, philologists, linguists, anthropologists, folklorists and literary scholars made inexhaustible efforts to investigate the time-tested folktales, folk epics, ballads, folk songs, proverbs, riddles, rituals and festivals and brought out their significance and intrinsic value. For their invaluable contributions to folklore studies and research, such names as the Grimm Brothers, Marian Cox, Antti Aarne, Vladimir Propp, Lévi-Strauss, Stith Thompson, C.W von Sydow, are remembered the world over. Furthermore, nobody can forget the significant role of the English Folklore Society, London, established in 1878, the American Folklore Society established in 1888 and the Finnish Literary Society established in 1831. Folklore programmes in the universities of the U.S. and Canada were introduced in the 1920s and the 1930s and thereafter M.A. and Doctoral degree programmes in folklore were established for the first time by Ralph Steele Boggs at the University of North Carolina, Chapel Hill, in 1940. Warren E. Roberts was the first American who received a Ph.D. degree in folklore from Indiana University in 1953. Indiana University had the first full-fledged Department of Folklore in America in 1963 under the aegis of Richard M. Dorson who succeeded Professor Stith Thompson after his retirement in 1955. Interestingly, Praphulladatta Goswami from the North East of India also got his D.Phil. degree in folklore from Gauhati University in 1955, and one of his examiners was Professor Stith Thompson. Goswami made a significant contribution to folklore studies in India by establishing the Department of Folklore Research at Gauhati University in 1972.

Folklore studies thus became a wide academic movement in the West in the 20th century, and in due course of time its influence reached other parts of the world. Many folklorists like Richard M. Dorson, Alan Dundes, Linda Degh, Felix J. Oinas, Warren E. Roberts, Dan Ben-Amos, Henry Glassie, W.E. Richmond, William R. Bascom and others gave strong directives on the development of folklore scholarship. In India Dr Jawaharlal Handoo took on the Herculean responsibility to arouse the minds of intellectuals, academics and students, injecting in them the importance of folklore studies, covering a wide range of this new field of knowledge from field collection to scientific study of Indian folklore. He visited all parts of this vast country, delivering lectures, holding seminars, symposiums and workshops for the promotion of folklore scholarship and research activities, opening departments and centres at many universities and institutions for about fifty years from the 1970s. Handoo, Founding father of Indian Folklore Congress (IFC) that has shown excellence for 43 years, has become a legendary figure of Indian folklore.

Among some of the problems encountered in the study of folklore in the Indian context, what saddens us most is the slow progress of folklore studies as a legitimate discipline in the universities and colleges. Apart from the general bias of the majority of Indian academics, the prevalent sweeping generalizations and simplistic attitude towards this discipline undermine the very spirit and temper of folklore studies. But nobody can veer away from this enchanting discipline and today we all know that without folklore we cannot know our past and our culture. Therefore, we have to revitalize the study of folklore and recognize its value. We have to respect it in its flesh and blood. Folklore is second to none as an academic discipline.

II

This volume contains papers contributed by Indian and Western folklorists. The response by Indian scholars represents the diverse views and very fundamental, distinct cultural expressions reflecting the particular while a few of the papers seek parallel traditions, yet available in cultures beyond ours. Although not all are trained and professional folklorists, their commitment and robust display of immediate cultural environment are by all means praiseworthy and insightful. The papers in this volume do not adhere to particular themes and genres; they are the personal reflections of the scholars on the issues taken up by them individually. Furthermore the limited number of the papers is strictly in accordance with the deadline given. Quite a few of the young scholars who have shown great interest in folklore research hopefully will forge ahead with furthering our accredited task. Our heartfelt thanks are due to the scholars from Estonia and the USA, Prof Ülo Valk, Head, Department of Estonian and Comparative Folklore, University of Tarto, Estonia, and Dr William Westerman, Department of Sociology and Anthropology, and Coordinator of the Program in Ethnic and Immigration Studies at New Jersey City University, respectively for their positive and timely response to our request to contribute to this volume.

In his paper, "Folklore in/ and Literature: Analogues and Orientations" Mani Meitei tries to show three things (i) the closeness of folklore and literary works, folklore being the provenance of written literature, (ii) an illustration of the structure of Fielding's *Tom Jones* patterned on the Proppian morphological structure, and (iii) how folkloristic elements such as myths, tales and proverbs have been used as literary devices and techniques in Chinua Achebe's novel *Things Fall Apart*. He argues that folklore is both a source and a means, not an end, that has been exploited in literary texts all through the ages. Interpretation of literary texts will never be banal if it is done through folklore in terms of patterns and designs on the one hand, and on the other hand if folklore is seen as a cultural paradigm to show the novelistic world as a challenge to the Eurocentric canons of literary formation especially when colonial discourse is dismantled in the postcolonial society, meaning that such folkloric elements serve as political means to reshuffle power relations. In order to illustrate these points Henry Fielding's *Tom Jones* and Chinua Achebe's *Things Fall Apart* are taken up for detailed study.

William Westerman in his paper, "Museums as Sites for Genocide Education: The Example of Chicago's National Cambodian Heritage Museum," makes a case study of a museum in Chicago, focusing on the Cambodian genocide in the 1970s. The paper addresses two functions of the museum. One is the more traditional educational function of the history of museum, educating the public about past events. In addition to this, museum focuses the educational work on preventing the recurrence of genocide in the future. The second function is healing for the community, by addressing the mental health needs of survivors as well as memorializing and acknowledging those who were killed during the genocide. It recounts the presence of a memorial room in the museum in addition to its gallery spaces and classroom. Thus, the paper underscores a re-examination of museums in the 21st century whether they are primarily repositories of tangible cultural heritage, or centres for education and dialogue around pressing cultural and social issues. At the same time, authoritarian leaders around the world are once again raising the possibility of genocide through their rhetoric.

"Blindness and Banishment in 'Rapunzel' and 'The Son of Seven Queens'" by Anjum Khan produces blindness and banishment, seen in folktales as sites for oppression unleashed on innocent people as a practice of torture prevalent in many societies, thus they correspond to social and cultural context. In both, disability is a kind of social ostracism, a disadvantage imposed, and the victim cut off from all. In order to demonstrate disability as a class by itself in the social hierarchy, Khan has brought two fairy tales into focus, one from *Grimm's Fairy Tales* and another from the storehouse of Indian folktales. The author delves into the problem of the disabled individuals in both the cases. In such tales, the disabled are socially excluded, and they undergo extremes of suffering and misery being themselves incapacitated as human beings. The seven queens and Rapunzel are a case in point. While demonstrating their miseries, what Khan observes is that they are not merely seen in the tales as fictitious characters and the happenings unreal but have tremendous social significance historicizing the oral source, which can be seen in terms of larger historical perspective inseparable from social and historical truths. Nonetheless such discourses are metaphors of human history and social truths.

"Rewriting Folk Narratives: A Case Study of Canadian Feminist Fantastical Voices" by Sumita Puri is an insightful new direction in the study of traditional oral narratives in the light of feminist subversion of the male oriented discourse which has remained by and large a site for power relations in which women are given a subordinate and insignificant role to reenact the prescribed gendered role by patriarchy. Myths, tales, fairy tales and fables are expressive of the biased views of society where women are eternally bound to their femininity, that is, to live up to the expectations of male ego. Represented as subservient to man to serve him through sacrifice, submission and as models of virtue, docility, sweetness, all to uphold man vision, she is a lost identity, never a full human being with a tendency to depend on man for her security, and living. Oral narratives are social and cultural documents which reflect the vicissitudes of life, hence very meaningful. This image of woman in oral narratives is no more fanciful than real in all probability. And this has done more harm than good towards structuring the social views on women which feminists reject by rewriting such stories from women's point of view in order to show that women are as potential as men. The appearance of women in man-made moulds is stereotypical rather than real. When such traditional stories are rewritten by feminists, women are more a class by themselves in a space of their own outside the century-old domestication and servitude.

Feminist rewriting is always an act of politics and is against the grain. Canadian feminist writers, Kaarina Kailo, Elizabeth Greene, Virginia Lee Hines, Paulin Pankin, Lorna Schwink, Francis Rooney, and others deconstruct the masculine voice in folk narratives and thus create an alternative discourse to unearth women's true worth. With this the traditional dichotomy between the sexes is reversed, decentred. Sumita Puri's study of the politically charged and revised folk narratives by Canadian feminist writers is as comprehensive as it is authoritative.

Tshering N. Bhutia points out some parallelisms between the Lepcha folk narratives and the Christian creation myth, the Tower of Babel and the Great Flood. In the Bible, the first human beings created by God were Adam and Eve who resemble Foodothing and Nazongnyo, also called Tukbothing and Nazeng Nyu, the first man and woman in the Lepcha creation myth. Their creator was not a God but a Mother Goddess, Itbu-Moo by name. Similar to the Biblical Tower of Babel, the Lepcha community has a mythical story about the construction of a high stair, Tallem Partam, going up to heaven but that crashes following some communication gap between the person on the top and the one at the bottom. Another narrative relates to a great flood like the Biblical one. As the level of water increased disastrously with little means to save the people, the Lepcha climbed the Tendong hill that raised its height which for the flood was unable to reach atop. The mythical connection of the Lepcha people in their narratives with the Biblical myths by way of similarities and parallelism later on helps convert them to Christians by Christian missionaries. Bhutia thus makes use of folklore for building religious sentiments through appropriation of ancient myth and legend.

Pragya Moirangthem in her paper "Gender Politics in the Manipuri Folk Epic *Khamba-Thoibi*" traces the origins of the world folk epics to the heroic age when heroic adventures and valour of great heroes were honoured as national pride, and models of conduct. Like many other folk epics, the Manipuri folk epic *Khamba-Thoibi* shows the dominating social order of patriarchal values where women are subjected to silence and obscurity, and their participation in social and cultural events is relegated to the margin, much to the displeasure of the heroine Thoibi. But unlike this general picture of women, Thoibi's stature as representing the articulate female voice is prevalent in the epic; that the epic does not move without her pivotal role always subversive, critical and judicious, such that the authoritarian patriarchal rule of the royal palace has to yield to her will many a time. She is an explicit feminist voice of protest in the folk epic, despite the strict patriarchal norms and the father's efforts to marry her forcibly with the man he chooses. Her true love for the hero Khamba never flickers in face of stiff opposition by her father. She accepts exile rather than living with Nongban. The paper interrogates gender politics and power relations, and the voice of the heroine as that of a liberated woman against the thick jungle of masculine power is heard. She chooses to be exiled and marries the man of her choice. The paper unravels social system as a villain which even makes a man villain while trying to meet social demands and expectations.

Cinderella tales are very popular all over the world with common motifs and characteristic regional or local cultural variants. In the paper "*Sandrembi Chaisra*, a Manipuri Cinderella: Global Character and Local Variants," S. Sanatombi gives a diachronic study of Cinderella tale types by European and American scholars, later by Chinese and Indian scholars. The variants are expressive of the cultural diversity the world over; for instance "O bird if indeed you're my queen, alight on my shoulder" appears in the Chinese, Indian and Korean oicotypes, and not in the European ones. Besides, she goes on to set her tale in this group, that is, the Asian Cinderella type where motifs like fish and turtle are commonly found as contrasted with the European cow or goat. Such versions become a highly fascinating side of Cinderella tales. Because of the characteristic presence of such motifs as substitution of the heroine by the step-sister, transformation of the heroine into a dove and a lemon tree (AT 408), Manipuri *Sandrembi Chaisra* becomes a combination of Cinderella AT510A and AT 408), that is Cinderella plus Three Oranges. Other cultural distinctions demonstrated in the study are fishing, marriage by abduction, post-marriage feast, belief in number seven and sword fight. The paper also makes an extensive study of three Cinderella tales, the Assamese *Teji and Teja*, the Manipuri *Sandrembi Chaisra* and the Myanmarese *The Big Tortoise*. Cinderella reveals cultural differences. Certain features of the Manipuri Cinderella are repeated killings of the heroine by her villainous step-sister, multiple transformations into a tortoise, a pigeon (AT 408: IV), then into a lemon tree (AT 408: v), and finally into a lemon fruit from which her earlier human form returns (AT 408: VI) to unite with the prince (AT 408: VII). Highlighting such common motifs and variants, the study examines the global and local elements in *Sandrembi Chaisra*.

Ülo Valk in his paper "Goddess Temples in North-Eastern India: Overcoming Narrative Distance in Place-Lore" devotes himself to the study of the ancient myths centring on deities and their overwhelming presence in two realms, one in the temple stories and another in the minds of the devotees, pilgrims and researchers who have received such stories as faith, truth—sacred truth. Ülo's paper has two distinct parts, the first being his scholarly display of the myth and legend theory in which he tries to formulate his own theory of myth, and the second is the narratology of his research experience and findings while he engaged himself as a field worker in the temples of Kamakhya goddess in Assam rediscovering the temple-lore, that enables to establish the timeless dimensions of the goddess, the shrines and other ritual practices that can remit the ray of the divinity to many a human heart. This is an attempt where he locates the trappings of his myth and temple theory incorporating it with the very narratives concerning the goddess. His well-rounded argument is focused on how the "deities are evoked through the art of storytelling and their sensible presence becomes possible through certain vernacular genres" and how "these generic qualities of certain narratives make people travel and seek the experience of the mythic realm." That through the discovery and retelling and rehearing such mythical stories, and the relics collected over the years, have established a reconnection between the ancient primeval world and this tangible world, is the hypothesis of this paper. A possible synthesis between two principles of truth, the transcendental and the temporal, is envisaged when the latter participates in the former, and both merge as a unique experience in the narratives involving "two distances—both in the geographical and narrative space." The profound influence from above is realized when we go beyond ourselves and be part of remaking process of such narratives still going on, oscillating as a pendulum between two distances of dream and reality. The paper is as much about myth as about negotiating the supernatural and its continual presence with the actual reality of lived experience.

In his paper "Oral History and Storytelling: Perspectives of the Chakmas," Pankaj Roy first accounts for the art of storytelling as the best way of expressing human emotions, experiences and it chronicles social, cultural and other phases of life. Before written history, storytelling became the history of people, the community, individuals, families, and so on. It is the history of the group or community where such tradition exists, and storytelling is the continuous process of reliving that history. Storytelling as a universal practice of folk traditions from the ancient times has been carried on, handed down from generation to generation ever since mankind started telling stories, myths, legends, folktales, ballads and folk epics. Oral stories are a constant source, not only of entertainment but also of knowledge and information pregnant with the past history of culture, traditions, practices, customs, beliefs, religion, worship, superstitions, and pragmatic ideas. Referring to the Chakmas, Roy says that the community history, their worldview, past and present are preserved in their oral narratives, stories, chants, incantations, superstitious beliefs, cultural norms and practices. To substantiate this, the paper recounts the Chakmas' songs, ballads, and other narratives long memoried in their community over the years. For instance, *Gyankhulee Gheet*, divided into thirteen *Palhas* (parts) composed in different historical times, was originally composed in the ancient period and describes the past life of the Chakmas in an entertaining way. *Vadya Pudhi*, a medicine man's book, is about the treatment of multiple forms of illness. It also deals with physical science, magical formulas, incantations, history of diseases and their symptoms, while throwing a great deal of light on the history of different deities, the manner in which they are to be worshipped to effect curing of many diseases. These traditional practices handed down through generations reveal Chakma life, lore and activities. They are an integral part of the oral life of the Chakmas, and explain and express strong emotions and experiences in memorable, long-lasting ways through the intricate use of rhythm, rhyme, and nuances of their culture. Such practices help preserve traditions, customs and societal standards, while bestowing immortality on leaders or ancestors. For the Chakmas, they form an important aspect of their community; through them they learn their own history, and they can render it into writing. Oral history gives history back to the people in their own words and in giving the past, it also helps them produce a future of their own making.

In the next paper "Mapping 'Arena Theatre': The Journey of 'Yatra' in Undivided Midnapore," Soumyadeep Chakraborty considers the multiple role played by the folk festival Yatra, a localized theatrical performance in West Bengal's Midnapore in the social, cultural, religious and political contexts. The classification based on the structure and presentation of Yatra into three main types with their distinctive characteristics expressing their different underlying motives and meanings has evoked multifarious designs and patterns of life, belief with or without social and cultural significance. Some of these Yatra forms have religious and social cohesive goals. On the whole, Yatra is a many-sided, collective and communal social, cultural activity with song and dance, and is both didactic and entertaining, bearing the identity of the culture. The paper argues that metaphorically, Yatra is both a journey of life and a strong medium of life and reality.

J.R. Meghana's paper "Indian and Arabic Folktales: An Overview" gives an account of Indian and Arab folktale collections like *Panchatantra*, *Jataka Tales*, *Akbar Birbal, Tenali Rama*, *Vikram Betal, Singhasan Battisi*, the *Arabian Nights* and *Hatim Stories*. The paper highlights the hallmark of the folktales, their significant social and cultural values and lessons imparted to people timelessly in their respective cultures in particular and mankind in general. They teach and guide human beings, the young and the old alike, through practical knowledge, wisdom and compassion propagated in them. The concepts of right and wrong, good and evil, love and hate, virtue and vice provide guidance to mankind.

Jayshree Singh's paper "Veer Rasa in the Heroic Ballads of Maharana Pratap" is concerned with the development in Rajasthani folklore of ballads dedicated to Maharana Pratap, the great scion of Mewar, who through his fierce spirit of freedom, invincible will to fight, unyielding heroic courage and valour not only defended his country against the mighty Mughal King Akbar but also sowed the seed of patriotism and nationalism emulated by future freedom fighters reminding them of "Hero-Worship." The heroic ballads that were composed in metrical verses singing praises of the hero of Mewar sprang from the native folk speech and rhythm of the folk conveniently conveying the theme and the subject-matter. These songs and lyrical ballads composed by poets on the valour and war theme are so distinguished by the typical metrical style with short stressed syllables and voiced plosive consonant sounds befitting the subject matter of heroic poetry, as exemplified in *Pracheen Rajasthani Geet*, for instance. Jayshree's critical linguistic analysis of the verses is an added strength of her paper. She posits that the toughness of the poetic rhythm and metrical structure of the Pingal language, combined with the lyrical perfection, can transmute the narrative in "Veer rasa" of Bharatamuni's *Natyashastra*—a poetic realization of a revered great warrior almost like God. Jayshree's main argument in the paper is that the rise of a genre in the folklore of Rajasthan based on the unrivalled valour, spirit of freedom and nationalistic and patriotic feelings of a great hero was a great deal due to the poets and bards who made use of such tribal and native languages and dialects as Pingal, Dingal commensurate with the very specific heroic theme and subject-matter. Sometimes the effect of the subject is achieved not because of the dialect or language but because of the folk rhythm and manner of folk speech patterns that convey the emotion and situational need similar to the evocation of the scene.

Jagadish Batra in his paper catalogues an array of proverbial, wise folk sayings all sung in couplets amongst the Haryanvi community. Such sayings or proverbs are composed in couplets in song form called *karke*. These songs perpetuate the long tradition current in the oral repertory of a folk community underlying the shared values and identity more homogeneously throughout the tradition of the group. The paper demonstrates how closely these folk songs are related to the community reflecting rural agricultural life, lore, beliefs and various aspects of their world whose activities centre round four good things, the possession of wheat, cow, good housewife, horse. Their community life is woven round crops, cattle, rainfall, famine, health and human relationships. Predictions and forebodings are not unknown in such sayings. Both entertaining and didactic, the role of such verse proverbs and wise sayings in the life of the rural folk is never to be overlooked for they are full of time-tested wisdom of the common people, laden with enlightening maxims, highly informative and educative. Further they act as an effective means of communication to drive home ideas which are not directly expressed, but then what is meant is easily conveyed. Professor

Batra argues that although they are current among the particular Haryanvi community, they cut across geographical and community lines and thus have universal imprint in them—set locally but the appeal is far more significant with universality. The paper reasserts that the very fabric of the agrarian community of Haryanvi lies nested in the traditionally handed down encapsulated, versified and multipronged proverbial expressions which act as patterns of folk life, and instruments of social control and raising awareness.

Lastly, we are inclined to respect each individual's opinions expressed in these papers. The papers included in this volume are not guided by a class of commonly chalked out theme or subject. Therefore they are all assorted topics on which the authors work independently. We are of the opinion that they are all scholarly and research-oriented papers where the observations are fresh and original. Further, we are hopeful that this collaborative volume will inspire academics and young Indian scholars to explore not only the diverse aspects of Indian folklore but also the local and regional folklore of India vis-à-vis world folklore. Though the papers are nowhere very specific about folklore theory as such, some of them are undoubtedly theory-oriented. Many of them are vehicles of the specificities of different cultures and societies. Multiplicity of folklore and folkloric genres and types makes the study of folklore ever-engrossing and the academic interest aroused by folklore and the searching minds of folklorists the world over will give us such a long journey of fertile attempts and hope of exploration hitherto not undertaken. All the contributors to this volume, from India and overseas, have partly done the spadework which is conducive to expand research and investigation. We owe our debt of gratitude to each one of them. Let a day come when a subsequent volume like this brings us together again.

Folklore in/and Literature: Analogues and Orientations

M. MANI MEITEI
Department of English and Cultural Studies
Manipur University

That folklore is not the fossil of dead traditions is a proven truth and that folklore dies out is not wholly true. Our oral traditions continue to exist in multiple channels of communication: oral narrative performances (myths, tales, legends, folk epics, proverbs, riddles, sayings, etc.), literary works, TV, radio, newspapers, magazines, email, internet, folklorismus shown in urban tourist centres, hotels, and in state, regional, national and international festivals. Apart from the type of folklore of prehistoric origins called "pure folklore," a new type of folklore, comparatively of recent origin, may be or has been found in some cultures and this type of folklore springs from created literary works, poems, songs etc. which is called "folklore of literary origin" (Propp 1984b: 9). Folklore is not a form of art acquired, or proliferated continuously for the enrichment of a culture, it has remained a vital organ of our culture and the folk are the bearers of traditions, beliefs and practices.

This paper will address, in the main, the inseparable relationship between folklore and written literature with illustrations, and then focus on the application of Proppian morphological analysis of the fairy tale to the novelistic form and structure of Henry Fielding's *Tom Jones*, patterned on the fairy tale structure, and then demonstrate how cultural myth, tales, beliefs, costumes, proverbs have been used as fictional devices and techniques by

Chinua Achebe in his world classic, *Things Fall Apart*. Achebe shows how these oral narratives play an important role in the social and cultural integration of Africa and how they can be an aspect of African writing today. With this in mind, he again teaches his people that their culture over the centuries has the power to sustain and cannot be tainted by the colonial (mis)representation: "I would be quite satisfied if my novels (especially the ones I set in the past) did no more than teach my readers that their past—with all its imperfections—was not a long night of savagery from which the first Europeans acting on God's behalf delivered them" (Achebe 1988: 45). While doing so I am not entering into the details of the differences between folklore and literature.

In one of his essays, Dundes expresses his doubt about any discussion having been made as to how an author has used folkloristic elements as literary devices, that is, how they function in literature:

> Too many studies of folklore in literature consist of little more than reading novels for the motifs or the proverbs, and no attempt is made to evaluate how an author has used folkloristic elements and more specifically, how these folklore elements function in the particular literary work as a whole. (Dundes 1979: 28)

Among the Western folklorists Dundes was one forward-looking scholar who made structural analysis of folklore, and delved into areas most of his predecessors and contemporaries either ignored or avoided. In part, this paper will be an approach to the neglected field of folklore research vis-à-vis literature.

Oral traditions, more especially oral literature, have long become the literature of the illiterate masses for countless number of years. And in many societies they continue to exist side by side with written literature as well. And such materials may be in purely oral form; some of them may even have been rendered into written form, yet still their status quo is maintained. On the subject of folklore and literature as sister arts, many scholars and folklorists have already written by devoting considerable time and energy. It is true that written literature has been immensely influenced by folklore. Literature and folklore are forms of verbal expression, and both are expressive verbal arts in the sense that their common medium is language. Folklore continues to exist mainly through verbal transmission, social, cultural and traditional practices, and media. Of the other forms of folklore, oral literature is highly considered an important organ of social and cultural life of peoples for its various constructive roles towards fulfilling a number of social needs. Through myths, tales, legends, proverbs and other forms of verbal expression, the collective life, history and civilization of a people have been created, recreated, conserved, preserved towards forming the group identity and worldview of the people. Each of these elements is informative, entertaining, or educative, and collectively they act to preserve the social and cultural and institutional values. Myth for instance has very useful function in our society. Malinowski argues:

> Myth fulfills in primitive culture an indispensable function: it expresses, enhances, and codifies belief; it safeguards and enforces morality; it vouches for the efficiency of ritual and contains practical rules for the guidance of man. Myth is thus a vital ingredient of human civilization; it is not an idle tale, but a hard-worked active force; it is not an intellectual explanation or an artistic imagery, but a pragmatic charter of primitive faith and moral wisdom. (Malinowski 1948, 1982: 101)

It is not that myth fulfilled that function in the primitive society alone and now it ceases to function that way; on the other hand, it "is not merely a story told but a reality lived. It is not of the nature of fiction . . . but a living reality, believed to have once happened in primeval times, and continuing ever since to influence the world and human destinies" (*ibid.* 100). In fact, cultural myths are very powerful safeguards of any given society, the image of man and life manifested in a myth is both sacred and sacrosanct, which time cannot wash out. Myth is the source of human faith, religion and a story of the origins of life. But in time myth is flanked by other outgrowths of culture of which other oral tradition genres but form an important ingredient. They appeared in diverse forms, songs, poems, narratives, tales, legends, proverbs, riddles, customs, traditions, performing arts, craft and architecture all of which are collectively called folklore belonging to all peoples with local, regional and national variants and differences. It is in this sense that William J. Thoms calls folklore "*the Lore of the People*" (Thoms 1965: 5), and its persistence to continue is a truism.

Folklore is a product of mass culture, but in contrast, literature is the product of the elite culture, the handiwork of an individual author who is in charge of the form, structure, content and style. Their distinction lies in the mode of authorship, transmission and medium of expression, for most forms originally folklore is orally transmitted although that is by no means the only one. There may be written form of folklore, then TV, radio, film, animated film, cartoon comics may be other modes of transmission as well, nor can we call all oral expressions. Likewise the printed form of folklore does not make it written literature. Conversely, even in literate societies orature continues to exist. We all share the view that folklore has remained a constant source of written literature, for literary artists have adopted various forms of folklore, themes, structure, and adapted stories to suit the artistic ends. Use of proverbs, myths, tales, legends, beliefs, superstitions, traditional and other practices is not uncommon. Writers from the Anglo-Saxon times down to the present day have drawn upon folklore and folkloric materials. We find the use of Arthurian legend, Robin Hood; Chaucer in his *Prologue to the Canterbury Tales* uses the oral narrative style; Shakespeare's plays are replete with folklore of different places, and so on. Homeric epics have inspired many literary artists the world over.

Literary artists generally do not use folkloric elements directly as they are but these are woven in the structure of the literary text, and thus add social, cultural and moral aspects to the very structure in the context of folkloric materials. Such materials also function as literary devices and techniques, and they also show the values of such traditions, customs and beliefs. J.M. Synge in his plays amply reveals the importance of these folk customs and traditions. In his *The Riders to the Sea*, Synge draws upon the native beliefs, superstitions, good and evil omens, traditional practices, beliefs, blessings, the significance of number in the peasant society of Ireland. They are tightly woven in the structure of the play; what happens in the play is orchestrated by these folk beliefs, customs and traditions. This displays how folklore has become inextricably an integral part of the life of the peasants of Aran Island. Synge's use of Irish myth, beliefs, superstitions, tales, legends and folk art revives the Irish life and retains folk rhythm, nuances and traditions, thus art recreates the lived life. Folkloric themes and mythical patterns are also frequently used for artistic purposes to show archetypal patterns and repeated events both in the heroic or mythical past and in the contemporary world as well, adding significance. Among the notable modern writers Eliot, Joyce and Yeats may be mentioned who make conscious use of mythical patterns in their works. Joyce's *Ulysses* is a "panorama" of the dilemma of the fragmented post-war state of the world where everything appears disjointed, but its structural design is influenced by the design of the *Odyssey* without which the protean world of Joyce would have been extremely inaccessible. He imposes a meaning on the formless chaotic world, represented in a unique style of the stream-of-consciousness fiction, a pattern through the journey and search motif as seen in *Ulysses* where Telemachus undertakes a journey in search of his father. Both Stephen and Leopold Bloom symbolically stand for Telemachus and Odysseus, and their experiences in the city of Dublin re-echo the design of the

Odyssey, but the subtlety of the design is that the kaleidoscopic experiences and encounters are subsumed into a diurnal setting. *Ulysses* is a parody of Homer's *Odyssey*. The use of Greek mythology and the design of the *Odyssey* in *Ulysses*, writes Eliot, "is simply a way of controlling, of ordering, of giving a shape and a significance to the immense panorama of futility and anarchy which is contemporary history. Instead of narrative method, we may use the mythical. It is a step toward making the modern world possible for art toward that order and form" (Eliot 1948: 123-24). Alan Dundes also elaborates on the use of a riddle in *Ulysses* based on identification and interpretation in the third chapter of his *Analytical Essays in Folklore* in which he studies the thematic significance of the riddle from psychoanalytical point of view. And this may be taken as a suitable methodology as to how the study of folklore in literature is to be carried out. It is not wise on the part of the literary critic to try to interpret a work of art without identifying the folkloric elements and their significant role. Equally undesirable is the attempt to identify such elements in a work of literature without properly interpreting the cultural context and functional values rendered by each element of folklore. Dundes calls to identify the motifs and types and other elements of folklore "objective and empirical" (Dundes 1979: 28) for that matter it is segregated from the cultural context, hence sterile. For full understanding of the cultural significance of a work of art "subjective and speculative" (*ibid.*) analysis or interpretation is preferable. Any study of folklore in literature must therefore be a revealing interpretation of the elements of folklore, the way they function in the work of art.

If we go on to study this aspect, scores of examples will be there. The Anglo-Saxon folk epic *Beowulf* is again an English epic derived from Scandinavian folklore, traditions, pagan mythology, conventions and code of conduct and quasi-historical facts. Because of their close proximity, at times it becomes a problem to distinguish folklore from literature and literature from folklore. Eliot's *The Waste Land* is again a good example of the meaningful use of cultural myth. From all this, it may rightly be inferred that folklore is the Ur form of literature whose subject-matter, form, structure, theme are provided by folklore. In the Indian context, many novelists writing in English have exploited the two epics, the *Ramayana* and the *Mahabharata*. Raja Rao, Anita Desai may be cited among others. Mythical elements abound in Girish Karnad's plays too.

About the relationship of folklore and literature or/and the literary use of folklore many folklorists have written a lot, and such a topic is no longer debatable. Theodor H. Gaster says: "folklore serves as a constant source and frame of reference for more formal literature and art; but it is distinct therefrom in that it is essentially of the people, by the people, and for the people" (Gaster 1984: 399). Simply because it is oral in character and so is its medium will not prevent the use of folklore in written literature for the reason that folklore is pre-eminent in the sense that before the birth of written literature folklore existed over thousands of years ago, hence as verbal art it is the precursor of literature. In many societies, the early history of literature is nothing but folklore—myths, ballads, tales, epics, songs, humour, jokes, riddles which are constituent elements of literature. Literature is not impervious to folklore. It is common knowledge that folklore is the progeny of many genres of written literature. For instance, "Myth contains germs of the future epic, romance, and tragedy; and it has been used in them by the creative genius of peoples and by the conscious art of civilization" (Malinowski 1984, 1982: 101). Archer Taylor points out three important things in regard to the relationship between folklore and literature: (i) Folklore is, in many cultures, indistinguishable from literature; (ii) literature contains elements borrowed from folklore; and (iii) writers have imitated folklore (Taylor 37). Because of their analogues it is hard to distinguish and draw a dividing line between literature and folklore; look at Old Testament, it is both "a book of traditions" and "the literature of the ancient Hebrews" (*ibid.*). We find Western literature comprising biblical elements very frequently. Their distinction lies in orientation: folklore looks backward, literature forward. Both are creative and innovative—each time the performer narrates stories he changes such stories creatively (Montenyohl 1996, 1998: 288). The earlier assumptions about the distinction of folklore and literature based on "ownership", "complexity," and "creativity" need to be revised. Propp argues, "Folklore is the product of a special form of verbal art. Literature is also a verbal art, and for this reason the closest connection exists between folklore and literature, between the science of folklore and literary criticism. Literature and folklore overlap partially in their poetic genres" (Propp 1984b: 5-6). Folklore infuses the soul into literature, a great deal. Dan Ben-Amos remarks: "From whatever perspectives historical, evolutionary, social, cultural, and artistic, folklore was regarded as the hand maiden of literature, its indispensable antecedent . . . of lower origins" (Ben-Amos 1982: 22). In this context, about the closeness of the two disciplines Jawaharlal Handoo writes, "folklore studies began to be considered a part of literary studies denying it the status of a separate discipline with its own distinct characteristics" (Handoo 1998: 4).

Many writers are very aware of the role of folklore and are influenced by the power of story-telling art, besides borrowing materials from oral traditions and narratives, myths, legends, tales and proverbs. We can record what Achebe tells once about the encouragement he got from an elder sister of his: "She told me many stories when I was young, and it was she who introduced me to the pleasure and art of story-telling" (Serraillier 1989). In some societies like the earlier Soviet Union, folklore is often identified with literature and the former was to glorify the latter. About the common identity of folklore and literature in the former Soviet Union, there is no doubt. Both have common national agenda, that is, the glorification of Soviet cultural unity.

In this part of the paper, first, I will bring into the light the structure of Fielding's *Tom Jones* approximating to the "empirical and inductive" framework of the fairy tale where, following Proppian synchronic structural model, there are thirty-one functions based on the characters' actions (functions). His study was based on the one hundred Russian fairy tales collected by Afáns'ev. This study will show the novel's structural analogues as identical with a fairy tale, that is to see the novel in the light of the morphological functions, arranged horizontally in their linear sequence, hence they show logical development of the actions of the dramatist personae. Propp says: "Functions of characters serve as stable, constant elements in a tale, independent of how and by whom they are fulfilled. They constitute the fundamental components of a tale" (1968, 1984: 21). The narrative of a tale constitutes these actions syntagmatically developed which "follow a logical sequence, and although no tale includes them all, in every tale the functions always remain in sequence" (Selden *et al* 1997: 72). The actor(s) and the actions followed in the form of a grammatical sentence with the divisions of subject as actor, and predicate as the typical actions conducted are so arranged syntagmatically based on the available signifiers at a point of time. Originally Propp's structuralism was restricted to the Russian fairy tales, but its method can be successfully applied to other forms of narrative, including myths, tales, epics, and literary texts in intra and cross-cultural context. This shows that by no means cultural patterns irrespective of their place to which they belong have commonly approachable routes. Propp's syntagmatic study has left out the paradigmatic parameters of cultural context, the latent, the absent structure underlying every social organization. Propp's theory therefore should be fertilized by the inclusion of Levi-Strauss's structural theory based on the latent social and cultural patterns towards finding meaning through the amalgamation of elements sharing the same function. While critically examining Propp's syntagmatic structure purely based on the logic of what Dundes calls "motif-hunting" and "word-counting" he (Dundes) contemplates the prime importance of cultural aspects in structuralism: "Whether this is so or not, there is certainly no reason in theory why the syntagmatic structure of folktales cannot be meaningfully related to other aspects of culture (such as social structure) (Dundes 1968, 1984a: xiii).

Novel writing in the West became a prestigious profession in the 18th century as the volume of reading public started to increase with the expansion of education, industrialization with which manual labour was a great deal replaced by machine. This led to the popularization of the art of novel writing in England. Novelists became more inclined to social realism, depiction of the middle class life, and activities of men and women in the social sphere. The created characters were to represent the vision and expectations of the people so that they would be identified with the characters. This was a means to steal the readers' thunder deviating them from the dull routine and domestic chores. Thus they could use the leisure time more profitably. People looked for comedy, romance, adventure, intrigues, and final denouement mainly through poetic justice. Stories were carved through the depiction of a likeable hero who would fall in love with a young beautiful heroine, misunderstanding or false projection of the hero would lead to his suffering. When the climax is reached, the mystery is revealed, crisis resolved, the villainy of the antagonist exposed further leading to the punishment of the wrong-doer, paving way for the happy marriage of the hero and heroine. This structure of the story followed widespread was modelled upon a fairy tale. It is this parameter through which Fielding's *Tom Jones* will be displayed only as part of this paper. Literary scholars are little aware of the structure of *Tom Jones* which is likened to that of a fairy tale.

However, before we proceed further we ought to know what we mean by fairy tale. Alexander Haggerty Krappe defines it in the following terms:

> By *fairy tale* we mean a continued narrative generally of a certain length, practically always in prose, serious on the whole, though humour is by no means excluded, centering in one hero or heroine, usually poor and destitute at the start, who, after a series of adventures in which the supernatural element plays a conspicuous part, attains his goal and lives happy ever after. (Krappe 1930: 1)

Furthermore, we have another definition slightly more elaborate than the above one:

> Fairy tales are episodic: the main character is separated from, or otherwise in trouble with, his or her family. He or she encounters severe or supernatural challenges and difficulties until, finally, all ends happily. Within this framework are set one or more extraordinary, usually magical, motifs, such as a character's ability to assume another shape, to come back from the dead, or to summon supernatural aid. Some fairy tales involve a quest for a spouse or for a magic object, some tell of a confrontation with an ogre or an evil human adversary, and some integrate magical motif into a humorous story. Typically, the tale is set apart from everyday speech with formulas such as "Once upon a time" and "They lived happily ever after." (Golberg 1998: 201-2)

Now let us see how far the structure of *Tom Jones* replicates that of the morphology of a fairy tale. Many of the thirty-one functions in Propp's model are available in a linear sequence in the novel. The following table will illustrate this analogue by way of a comparison:

Propp's function	Structural function of *Tom Jones*
I. One of the members of a family absents himself from home: (b.).	"Mr. Allworthy has been absent a full quarter of a year in London on some very particu-

		lar business" (Fielding 1966: 5).
II.	An interdiction is addressed to the hero: (y.).	Finding Tom good, generous and honourable Allworthy asks him to be prudent and religious meaning to obey social norms and decorum.
III.	The interdiction is violated; entry into the scene a Villain: (d.).	Tom's moral depravity—his association with Black George, little acts of mischief here and there—causes concern. Hence the Black George may be treated as a villain let alone Blifil. Both damage and harm Tom's reputation.
IV.	The villain makes an attempt at reconnaissance; Reconnaissance: (e.).	Blifil is all the time spying on Tom.
V.	The villain receives information about his victim: (f.).	Blifil gets information that Tom was with Black George, the gamekeeper, when the partridge was shot. He also collects information about Tom and Sophia affair.
VI.	The villain attempts to deceive his victim in order to take possession of him or of his belongings: (n.).	Earlier on Blifil slips the string from the leg of Sophia's bird (presented by Tom) and sets it free. This is an act of disapproval of what Tom does.
VII.	The victim submits to deception and thereby unwittingly helps his	Tom is vociferous, noisy by which he incurs the wrath of Blifil; his roaring drunkenness

	enemy: (z.).	and fight with Blifil when Allworthy is ill unwittingly help his enemy.
VIII.	The villain causes harm or injury to a member of a family: A7 Villainy: the villain causes a sudden disappearance: (A.).	Blifil dismisses the attorney who comes from Salisbury to meet Mr. Allworthy. Thus Blifil casts a spell upon Allworthy.
VIIIa.	One member of a family either lacks something or desires to have something: (A.).	Tom lacks prudence, tact and bride, love; he lacks means of existence.
IX.	Misfortune or lack is made known: the hero is approached with a request or command: he is allowed to go or he is dispatched: (B.).	Tom is summoned, dismissed and exiled by Allworthy from home, and the story is linked to his fate (victimized hero). The banishment of Tom leads to the disappearance of Sophia from Squire Western's horizon, and the father goes off in search of his daughter, then the father is called (seeker hero).
X.	The seeker agrees to or decides upon counteraction: (C.).	.
XI.	The hero leaves home: (&.).	There are two types of heroes, the seeker-hero and the victim-hero. The first would confine himself to search, while the latter would start "a journey without searches, on which various

		adventures await the hero" (Propp 1968, 1984a: 39). On the way Tom fights with rowdy soldiers and gets wounded being treated by a local barber; fights with Northerton on the Gloucester Road, picks up Mrs Waters from Worcester to spend the night with her at Upton Inn. He scuffles with Mr Fitzpatrick. Sophia arrives and gathers that Tom is in bed with a woman, quits immediately after leaving her muff. Tom follows her to London.
XII.	The hero is tested, interrogated, attacked, etc. which prepares the way for his receiving either a magical agent or helper: (D.).	Tom is tested, attacked, and he also gets help from unexpected donors so that he can reach London. On the way Tom collects Sophia's pocket book and a bank-bill of 100 pounds from a lame beggar. His meeting with a highwayman further helps him reach London safely. These people act as donors. More donors are yet to come.
XIII.	The hero reacts to the actions of the future donor: (E.).	In London Tom takes lodgings to the home of Mrs Miller, whose daughter Nancy in love with Mr Nightingale is helped by convincing the father of Nightingale, thus he brings the two families together ending

		the suffering of Mrs Miller.
XIV.	The hero acquires the use of magical agent: (F: D^8E^8 F^8).	Tom loses all his chances of recovery. He falls into the clutches of Lady Bellaston. Further he is accused of murder and is in jail awaiting his death by hanging. He is accused of incest with his own mother. Such crimes are never to be pardoned in a civilized society. All this seems quite different from the heading of the function on the left side, but the points raised can be part of the sub-headings (F: D^8E^8 F^8).
XV.	The hero is transferred, delivered or led to the whereabouts of an object of search: (G.).	This function comes later. Tom's object of search in London is Sophia whom he finds in a theatre, and promises to reform.
XVI.	The hero and the villain join in direct combat: (H.).	At this crucial hour it is not his mortal antagonist, Tom fights, but Mr Fitzpatrick who finds Tom with his wife when the latter goes to her for advice as he is to lose Sophia to Blifil (when Sophia's father and Squire Allworthy and Blifil arrive in London for the villain's marriage).
XVII.	The hero is branded: (J.).	It is not the hero wounded but it is he who wounds Mr Fitzpatrick. The hero is immedi-

	ately hustled off to jail.
XVIII. The villain is defeated: (I.).	The villain is defeated (falsely pronounced dead). The villain may not necessarily be the same, but may appear in many forms different from the earlier one.
XIX. The initial misfortune or lack is liquidated; lack liquidated: (K.).	This is not an act of liquidating the villain but only seemingly so because the villain here is some sort of trouble monger.
XX. The hero returns: (@.).	
XXI. The hero is pursued: (Pr.).	In many ways the hero is pursued (i) by Sophia up to a point, (ii) by Lady Bellaston, (iii) conversely by Mrs. Waters for help.
XXII. Rescue of the hero from pursuit: (Rs.).	Except in the initial stage, the hero is no more pursued, although he is on a journey of self-discovery.
XXIII. The hero unrecognized; arrives home or in another country unrecognized arrival: (o.).	Tom comes to London unrecognized by Sophia, and others.
XXIV. A false hero presents unfounded claims; unfounded claim: (L.).	Blifil declares that Tom killed Mr Fitzpatrick (so that his earthly obstacle is finally removed by his death).
XXV. A difficult task is proposed to the	In this case the difficult task the hero is to perform is to prove

hero: (M.).	himself that he is innocent. He cannot do it himself but his donors will help him.
XXVI. The task is resolved: (N.).	While waiting for his doomsday, the hero is helped by his friends and acquaintances: it is Mrs Miller who shows up to tell Squire Allworthy that it was not Tom's fault to have the duel with Mr Fitzpatrick (a fact which Mr Fitzpatrick himself on recovery from his wound, graciously acknowledges); Mrs Waters discloses to Allworthy that she is not the mother of Tom Jones, but the real mother was his sister Bridget; she informs Allworthy that on her deathbed Bridget left a message with Blifil concerning Tom's parentage, and Blifil had treacherously destroyed it; she also tells Allworthy that Blifil bribed the witnesses to get Tom hanged for the duel with Mr Fitzpatrick even though the gentleman had not died of the wounds. Thus the difficult task is resolved.
XXVII. The hero is recognized: (Q.).	Tom is recognized not by means of a scar, a ring, or by some difficult task or after a long period of separation, but

	by the discovery of his true worth, good nature, and re-morse.
XXVIII. The false hero or villain is exposed: (Ex.).	With the recognition of the true worth of Tom, the villain Blifil is exposed.
XXIX. The hero is given a new appearance: (T.).	The task of the helpers is to discover the concealed identity of the hero (Tom) so that a "new appearance is directly ef-fected" (Propp 1968, 1984a: 62) as if by magic.
XXX. The villain is pun-ished: (U.).	Blifil is stripped of his false claim, punished and removed from the scene on a yearly sti-pend.
XXXI. The hero is married and ascends the throne: (W.).	Once the true worth of Tom is discovered, he inherits Allwor-thy's wealth and properties as the true heir. Tom marries Sophia.

This method of analysis of *Tom Jones* is purely based on the synchronic distribution of the functions of the dramatist personae and has eschewed literature's concern with cultural context. What is the most crucial point raised in Proppian model is that a literary work has a coherent structure of its own, an experiment to demonstrate how characters in a fictional work relate to each other by way of functions they display interlocking all actions and interactions as the plot moves towards its climax. It is pure art in which we can see a two layered-structure, the outer and the inner, the visible and the invisible design. The application of Proppian method is to see the inner design of a work like paint-ing in which we perceive a pattern underlying a text. It is intriguing that *Tom Jones*' outer framework is an analogue of fairy tale structure. "Propp approaches," argue Jason and Segal, "the problem of plot structure as a tool to find an extra-textual linear model which would both provide a semantics of the plot and a genetics of the fairy tale" (2). Thus Propp's structuralism questions the treatment of literature as a vehicle of the author's humanistic, moral and spiritual views for literature has no other truth function outside the immediate linguistic structural units that work by combination of such elements in a sequential order.

Of the various ways in which folklore has been used in literature, one example will be how Achebe has used his cultural/ folkloric materials as novelistic techniques—myths, rituals, tales, proverbs, songs, jokes and other social practices such as the village crier giving message to the villagers, on the one hand, and then, as a social and political propaganda subverting the colonial discourse in the struggle for political self-determination and cultural self-identity by which the colonized people would be able to reconstruct their lost past, on the other hand. It is because of this the role of folklore is great in postcolonial literature, be it Indian, or African. Chinua Achebe and Raja Rao in their novels, *Things Fall Apart* and *Kanthapura* respectively, are examples. Many of Achebe's contemporaries, Amos Tutuola, Soyinka, Ekwensi, Okara, Ngugi are iconic African writers and they have made use of their oral traditions and folklore to represent their African life, culture, ethos, experiences and worldview, more especially as anti-colonial discourse. They along with a number of African women writers could construct and formulate African aesthetics.

Achebe's magnum opus *Things Fall Apart* is replete with oral traditions, social folk customs, beliefs, superstitions which are not only socially and culturally important but also they are the structural props of the novel in question. The novel's plot development, the rise and fall of the protagonist which reecho Greek tragedy are punctuated with the African myths, legends, beliefs, superstitions, rites, proverbs, and so on. In this context, we can single out a few events to illustrate the role of these folkloric elements.

For instance, the fall of Okonkwo from a great culture hero to a despicable man is linked to his violations of cultural norms, disobedience of the Oracle of the Hills and the Caves and the Goddess Ani. First, he violates the Week of Peace by beating his third wife, followed by the killing of Ikemefuna against strong warning that he should not bear a hand in his death, and then his inadvertent gun-firing in which Ezeudu's son is killed. Such crimes were seldom committed in the past for fear of the clan's misery. His fear of being dubbed a weak man makes him turn a blind eye to all until he is isolated from all. For such crimes a man would be denied his burial place. He goes into hiding for seven years in his mother's land where he admits "Mother is Supreme," thus his self-image is considerably weakened. The book's mythical structure is to impose a comprehensive form and order on the depiction of African communal life vis-à-vis Okonkwo. Gradually Okonkwo is dehumanized as the novel progresses from the first part to the third part exacerbated by Western colonization. As the protagonist falls from grace to ignominy, the culture also gives way to Christianity.

Achebe is praised for his mastery over the use of proverbs. African proverbs are very significant in the lives of African people, "Negro proverbs constitute one of the most potent factors for individual conformity and cultural continuity. In West Africa proverbs are cited in court trials in much the same way the European lawyers cite cases of which serves as legal precedent. (Waterman and Bascom 1949, 1984: 22). Achebe says: "Among the Ibo the art of conversation is regarded very highly, and proverbs are the palm-oil with which words are eaten" (Achebe 1958, 1989: 6). In Africa "Almost never does a discussion lack the spice of proverbs" (Waterman and Bascom 23). And the high place of proverb in African society is once more confirmed:

"The Chaga have four big possessions: land, cattle, water, and proverb" (*ibid.*).

An examination of the proverbs reveals the novel's plot has ever been carried through with so consummate skill along the path of the rise and fall of Okonkwo's tragic fate wherein the proverbs are but a commentary on the various stages of the culture vis-à-vis Okonkwo, surrounded by forebodings he is not aware of, although his culture cries. Achebe makes his culture a living being that foresees the doomsday. We can see some of the well-crafted proverbs: "if a child washes his hands he could eat with kings" (7) and "Okonkwo had clearly washed his hands and so he ate with kings and elders" (*ibid.*) indicate without elaborate description Okonkwo's especial and elevated place in his culture. "Looking at a king's mouth one would think he never sucked at his mother's breast" (23) means that becoming a successful man entails hard work, even extreme hardships; "A toad does not run in the daytime for nothing" (19) reappears in the mouth of Okika, in a big gathering much later when crisis engulfs Umuofia following the arrest of six village leaders including Okonkwo, "Whenever you see a toad jumping in broad daylight, then you know that something is after its life" (178). The first is a talk about Obiako, a palm-wine tapper, who suddenly gives up his trade as a result of a warning by the Oracle that he would fall off a palm tree. The second refers to the present state of Umuofia which would fend itself, or else the future of the land is at risk. Every stage of the novel's plot development is shown by such proverbs. The impending danger in which Umuofia is caught up is expressed by the use of animal imagery, "Umuofia was like a startled animal with ears erect, sniffing the silent, ominous air and not knowing which way to run" (173). The simile is so powerful that without any description or explanation it hints at the present state of the land. One can easily perceive the narrative function of the proverbs in *Things Fall Apart* that by the economical use of these the novel casts a spell over the readers the world over and thus sets an example for others to emulate. Their function is to harness the plot movement from high fortune to low fortune through the errors and blind arrogance of the protagonist, much to the annoyance of both man and god. The twin purpose of these proverbs is explicit, one the narrative strategy they take, and another, the enhancement of the meaning of the novel only when the cultural context is taken into account. Thus proverbs themselves become a hallmark of *Things Fall Apart* because the setting, characterization and the very structure of the novel are coherently cemented within the oral repository of African culture.

Throughout the novel, Achebe tries to capture the attention of the reader by recourse to his culture, and fulfils what Forster calls, "what would happen next." Suddenly when the whole village is in sound sleep the silent air is rent, "Gome, gome, gome, gome, boomed the hollow metal. Then the crier gave his message. . . . Every man of Umuofia was asked to gather at the market place tomorrow morning" (9), the village crier would shout. This technique gives anxiety, suspense and curiosity about what would happen, some war, conflict, death or disaster or misfortune. In this case Achebe uses folk media as a narrative technique in his novel. Sometimes the priestess of Agbala is assigned to do that terrifying nightly rite. Achebe's native inclination to plunge into the traditional practices is to heighten the novel's effect on the reader through folk medium. This is for the purpose of giving a new accent to his readers.

Things Fall Apart is basically an unconventional novel. Himself a first-rate storyteller, Achebe follows the art of a tale teller. The book itself reads like a folktale: amusing events, a number of gods, goddesses, battles, spirits, beliefs, superstitious, customs, description of seasons, rites, religion, birth, marriage, death, social and family ties all reinforcing the communal life of his culture. It recreates African history, the pre-colonial, and the colonial. The tale of a tortoise he narrates—an etiological one -

suggests the basic theme of the novel—the racial conflict, the clever tortoise that exploits the innocent birds is the white colonizer or missionary, and the birds the simple natives. This has reference to the wiping off of the Abame tribe by the whites. Again the story of a mother kite and its daughter, the latter of which catches a duckling, whose mother just does not put up a fight means a curse on the daughter kite, has a direct moral bearing on the underlying theme of the book, and the end of Okonkwo, who is cursed for killing the silent and innocent boy Ikemefuna, who calls him father. Obierika cautions him: "What you have done will not please the Earth. It is a kind of action for which the goddess wipes out whole families" (58). The death of Okonkwo by hanging himself following his killing of the messenger is reconnected with the earlier curse that he would not be given a burial place by the Earth Goddess. As a tradition, a person who dies by hanging is not given a burial place in Umuofia.

Besides it being a critique of his culture, *Things Fall Apart* is an anti-colonial discourse. In it there is the resistance of the natives against the white rule that dislocates the century-old African culture. Look at the Ibo folk song:

> *Kotma* of the ash buttocks,
> He is fit to be a slave.
> The white man has no sense,
> He is fit to be a slave. (154)

This may be regarded as a political song sung during political struggle for independence in a colonized society. It tries to reverse the power of the colonizer while he is put in the position of the colonized. The song implies the technique of mimicry in postcolonial writing which at one time is "poking fun" while at the other camouflaging therefore unmasking the dominating power of the colonizer. It creates fun at the cost of the colonizer. Nigeria came under British rule in 1900 and got independence in October 1960. During national liberation movements it was not uncommon to use folksongs as a political tool of mass consciousness (it was a practice in China and India as well, for instance). In his article "Music as Agent of Political Expression," Willard Rhodes "discussed a number of songs that were employed in Africa to promote anti-colonialism, nationalism, regionalism, and Pan Africanism in the period leading up to 1960, when so many African states gained independence" (Bascom 1981: 213).

Thus we witness *Things Fall Apart* as a model of modern use of folklore in literature with social, cultural, literary, political implications. The social, cultural and political orientations of the novel are so unique owing to meaningful and authentic use of folkloric materials per se. These are some of the examples I have singled out in this study.

My intention in this paper was to show the closeness of folklore and literature, especially the contribution of folklore to literature, and mainly to the understanding of literature through culture. Folklore as a material of literature and as the pulse of the people will remain a fertile area for future research and scientific investigation.

Bibliography

Achebe, Chinua. *Hopes and Impediments*. New York: Anchor Books, 1988, 1990.

_____. *Things Fall Apart*. Oxford: Heinemann, 1958, 1989.

Bascom, William R. *Contributions to Folkloristics*. Meerut: Archana Publications, 1981.

Ben-Amos, Dan. *Folklore in Context: Essays*. New Delhi: South Asian Publishers, 1982.

Dundes, Alan. *Analytical Essays in Folklore*. The Hague: Mouton, 1979.

_____. "Introduction" to the Second Edition of *Morphology of the Folktale* by V. Propp.

_____. *The Study of Folklore*. New Jersey: Prentice Hall, 1965.

Eliot, T.S. "Ulysses, Order and Myth," *Forms of Modern Fiction*. Ed. William van O'Connor. Minneapolis: The University of Minnesota Press, 1948.

Fielding, Henry. *Tom Jones*. 2 Vols. London: Dent, 1966.

Gaster, Theodor H. "Folklore," *Standard Dictionary of Folklore, Mythology, and Legend*. Ed. Maria Leach. San Francisco: Harper and Row, 1949, 1984.

Golberg, Christine. "Fairy Tale," *Encyclopedia of Folklore and Literature*. California: ASC-Clio, 1998.

Handoo, Jawaharlal. *Folklore: An Introduction*. Mysore: CIIL, 1989.

Jason, Heda and Dimitri Segal, eds. *Patterns in Oral Literature*. The Hague: Mouton, 1977.

Krappe, Aleaxander Haggerty. *The Science of Folklore*. London: Methuen, 1929.

Malinowski, Bronislow. *Magic, Science and Religion*. London: A Candor Book, 1948, 1982.

Montenyohl, Eric. L. "Folklore and American Literature," *American Folklore: An Encyclopedia*. Ed. Jan Harold Brunvan. Library of Congress Cataloging-in-Publication Data 1996, 1998.

Propp, Vladimir. *Morphology of the Folktale*. Trans. Laurence Scott. Texas: University of Texas Press, 1968, 1984a.

_____. *Theory and History of Folklore*. Trans. Ariadna Y. Martin and Richard P. Martin and several others. Manchester: Manchester University Press, 1984b.

Selden, Raman, Peter Widdowson, Peter Brooker. *A Reader's Guide to Contemporary Theory*. London: Prentice Hall, 1997.

Serraillier, Ian. "Introductory Note" to *Things Fall Apart* by Chinua Achebe. Oxford: Heinemann, 1958, 1989.

Taylor, Archer. "Folklore and Student of Literature," *The Study of Folklore*. By Alan Dundes. New Jersey: Prentice Hall, 1965.

Thoms, William J. "Folklore," *The Study of Folklore* by Alan Dundes. New Jersey: Prentice Hall, 1965.

Waterman, Richard A. and William R. Bascom. "Africa and New World Negro Folklore," *Standard Dictionary of Folklore, Mythology, and Legend*, ed. Maria Leach. San Francisco: Harper and Row 1949, 1984.

Museums as Sites for Genocide Education: The Example of Chicago's National Cambodian Heritage Museum

WILLIAM WESTERMAN
Department of Sociology and Anthropology
New Jersey City University

The last few decades have seen the commitment of museums to doing more than simply displaying artifacts of interest. History and memorial museums, and places known as historic "sites of conscience," have taken the educational initiative in telling the stories of genocides or mass murders or crimes against humanity. There have been most famously memorials to the European Holocaust, but not exclusively, as history is replete with examples of hatred and ignorance leading to violence against innocent civilians. As schools and educational institutions move towards simply preparing youth for the labor force, other cultural institutions must assume the mantle of providing educational resources about ethical behavior and human history.

The Cambodian American Heritage Museum and Killing Fields Memorial, as it was known when it was founded in Chicago in October 2004, has a unique mandate: to serve the Cambodian community as a site of reconciliation and healing, and to serve both the non-Cambodian public and the younger American-born generation by educating them about Cambodian culture and history. When it was founded under their auspices, the Cambodian Association of Illinois, a local social service agency (or

Mutual Assistance Association) then led by Mr. Kompha Seth, had the intention to educate the general public about all of Cambodian history. But it was obviously the years of the Khmer Rouge regime, 1975-1978, and the stories of refugee survivors in Chicago that became the central focus, largely because that was the reason 150,000 Cambodians came to the U.S. There was another Cambodian museum founded privately in Tacoma, Washington, around the same time, but the museum in Chicago was the first museum founded by a Cambodian community association and incorporated over twenty other ethnic and immigrant museums in Chicago. The Cambodian Association raised funds and was able to build an extension onto their office building, adding gallery and memorial space, and office, and a library and archive of books and published works on Cambodian history and culture.

The standard concept of the Museum, not just in the U.S. but throughout the museum profession worldwide, is changing. Museums such as this one are leading the way, developing into educational and civic institutions and not just repositories of valuable property, antiquities, and other curios. They aim to serve the entire community, and not just the elite social classes.

What Seth, an ethnic Khmer from Surin, Thailand, who immigrated to the U.S. before the genocide, envisioned was that a museum can be a site of education, of course, but also healing. Because of the trauma involved in the Khmer Rouge experience, Cambodian refugees were found in a 2005 study to have widespread ongoing mental health issues decades later: 62% exhibiting PTSD and 51% experiencing clinical depression in the prior year (Marshall et al. 2005). Thus, educating the public becomes a mechanism, strategy, and rationale for the community to not only represent itself, but begin a discussion about healing. Not least in this process is the possibility for opening up intergenerational conversation, as it is common in genocide survivor communities for the survivors not to discuss any of what they went through with their offspring. Anyone born after 1979 would not have experienced the genocide, though they might have been born or raised in refugee camps in Thailand.

Genocides, unless one comes from the persecuted group, are too quickly forgotten. Sadly, in a very real sense, for anyone born outside of Cambodia after 1985, the genocide is ancient history, especially compared to current conflicts as well as more recent genocides in Rwanda and Bosnia in the early 1990s, Darfur beginning in 2003, and ongoing, devastating wars in Syria and Afghanistan that have produced millions of refugees. The university groups that come through the Museum with a hundred percent recognition of Cambodia and the Khmer rouge were the exception, not the norm, and those were only in cases when teachers had specifically prepared them for the field trip. Most younger students and most college students come to visit with no knowledge of the genocide.

I was not present in Chicago during the development and founding of the Museum (I am actually from neither Chicago nor Cambodia), but was brought in several months later as a consultant and eventually became the museum's first director in 2005-6. There I worked alongside our museum educator, Mr. Ty Tim, a respected teacher in Cambodia who had spent his first twenty years in the U.S. amassing a personal archive of Cambodian history and culture in his own home. I write about the early days of the Museum, which has since gone on to incorporate on its own under the new name of National Cambodian Heritage Museum. At the time, the Museum committee chair was a high school teacher and assistant principal (who also happens to have been a Killing Fields survivor and a medic in the refugee camps), Leon Lim. From his perspective, the ideal audience for the Museum's exhibits and educational programs were high school and college students. In fact, students at the high school where he taught developed a genocide education curriculum under their service-learning program. This curriculum, which ran nearly 125 pages, became the early cornerstone of our high school education program, and, since the school was a selective magnet high school, was suitable for use at colleges as well. But both Lim and I, at the time, were surprised by elementary school groups that have visited, including one remarkable group of 1st-3rd grade after-school students who had been well prepared in advance by their teachers. The sad and in some ways ironic truth is that many of the killers in Cambodia were elementary school-age as well, and this was a tragic point we could make with their teachers for follow up.

This presents a challenge to the mission of Museum education that goes beyond most museum education programs, which tend to be limited in depth and ambition. For one thing, a Museum such as this has to have a strong adult educational component. Furthermore, we believed it was insufficient to educate students without also educating teachers to carry on this education in the classroom, and organizing teachers to develop their own genocide curricula that may not be based at the Museum.

But the need to know about genocide in Cambodia, and more broadly as a human phenomenon, doesn't stop at one's graduation, nor does museum education stop at the museum's door. Most museums, in my experience, see the education department as being geared almost entirely toward school-aged populations, and neglect very important work that can be done in adult education. In fact, through my prior experience as a museum director of a local history museum in another state, I developed an adult popular education program yet was criticized by the board for neglecting the museum's educational mission. Education is not just for children but is still too often seen that way, even by too many local museum boards.

One thing I learned early on was that it would be a big mistake for us to assume prior knowledge or understanding of complex genocides in the last century. As a university-level educator since leaving the Museum, I became even more aware of this, in both private and public universities. American society—which is by no means alone in this regard—lacks knowledge about the causes and extents (not to mention the existence) of genocides in Guatemala, Bosnia, Rwanda, Iraq, Bangladesh, and so on. As Samantha Power aptly demonstrated in her 2002 classic text, *A Problem from Hell,* the United States government's lack of interest in getting involved to stop genocide is buttressed by Americans' lack of knowledge and understanding of current events. This is in addition to, I would add, a tendency not to look at root causes or instead to take an ahistorical approach, a tendency which has only increased since the generation that came of age in the 1960s.

High school U.S. history, at least from what I have heard from my students who come from dozens of local high schools, rarely covers the War in Southeast Asia (usually called the Vietnam War), and there are very few schools where Asian history is taught alongside U.S. and European history, of particular disappointment to Asian-American students. Though the Cambodian genocide under the Khmer Rouge is relatively well-known compared to others, or perhaps emblematic of the most extreme form of Communism, there is less knowledge of the years of famine afterwards (that is, 1979 to 1982), and even less awareness among visitors to the Museum of the extent of the American bombing and the Civil War from 1970 to 1975, an issue of particular importance to the leaders of the Cambodian Association. That the period could be broken up into three phases—the U.S. bombing from 1970 to 1975, the Khmer Rouge regime and social transformation from 1975 to 1978, and the Vietnamese overthrow, subsequent fighting, and famine, from 1979 to 1982—is barely recognized. The fact that at least 500,000 people had already been killed during the civil war and U.S. bombing, as audiences learned at a symposium sponsored by the Museum on refugee mental health, is virtually unknown.[1]

Furthermore, there are very few museums that would take on the kind of community-based public program that Kompha Seth initiated in his role as director of the Cambodian Association of Illinois, which we then situated in the museum's main gallery space. It was congruent with our sense that the museum was there not just to serve those who did not know about the genocide, but also to provide education-based services to those survivors in the community who would benefit from discussion of the issues of trauma that have long-lasting repercussions.

This in itself would put the Cambodian Museum in the same category as the U.S. Holocaust Memorial and other "sites of conscience" around the world: those few cultural institutions whose charge it is to commemorate the victims of these crimes against humanity. Because commemoration is healing. You are not just commemorating for third parties, but sometimes the creation of a greater memorial consciousness helps survivors by validating their strength and the challenges they have faced and continue to face. This is all new territory in the history of museums.

When we organized a workshop for educators interested in teaching about genocide, I chose to begin the program with talks by survivors of genocide in Cambodia, Guatemala, and South Sudan, which at that point was not yet an independent nation but which had a significant refugee presence in Chicago at the time. All the evaluations came back indicating that the first-person narratives were the highlight of the day. Personally I think that kind of cross-cultural encounter is an irreplaceable method of retelling history and turns audience members, in this case teachers, into a kind of participatory observers. I also acknowledge the problematic situation of asking survivors of trauma to perform their narratives for outsiders, even by those who are willing or who are engaged in this as a therapeutic exercise. But Museums can become sites where these first-person narratives, alternative tellings of history from the point of view of those in minority, colonized, indigenous, and immigrant communities, can be told and heard across cultural divides. This changes the concept of a museum from a static repository of objects to a living and interactive cultural space, one that is a permanent institution, which would otherwise be lacking except in more ephemeral formats. Slowly museums around the world are waking up to this mission.

In 2005, Illinois became the second state (after New Jersey) to require the teaching of genocide education beyond the European Holocaust in elementary and secondary schools. Yet this unfunded mandate was also unpromoted; one teacher at our teachers' workshop indicated the first she had even learned of this requirement was through our postcard invitation to this workshop. So one of our tasks, in addition to providing basic genocide education, was to serve as an organizing body to bring teachers together and provide them with resources that they can use. This is something I suggest we can do as a cultural institution more easily than a school. Universities can also do this, but paradoxically may not have the funds available to do so, especially as budgets tighten and programs for students only are given priority over programs to benefit the entire community.

This organizing function of education programs at museums is consistently overlooked, although it has been present at a number of folk arts organizations with which I have been associated. Education can be the imparting of a base of knowledge or material, or it can be, in the Freirean sense (1970), the arena for a critical questioning and examination of the material conditions of people's lives or of nature. But museums, as semi-formal institutions of learning, have an additional role to play in which they can bring together educators from across geographic and disciplinary boundaries as well as across age-level groups, to expand the agenda of questions with which teachers and students are customarily concerned. Museum educators can set agendas, frame problems, and above all provide what I would call deep resources in the form of exhibits, audiovisual materials, artifacts, texts, and community contacts. (Conceivably, even organizing international tours, which museums do all the time, could be part of genocide education.)

This idea of organization is particularly important in primary and secondary education. University workshops on human rights education at the college level in the U.S. are far more common than such workshops offered for secondary school educators. The problem as I saw it was that, by the time many students select their place and course of post-secondary education, the option of following a human rights curriculum may be already shut out for them if the school does not offer that, or in countries where the educational track in universities is limited to a particular course of study. (Can a class or paper in human rights, for example, be available to Indian students of commerce? It often depends on the university of which a college may be a constituent.) To my surprise, Illinois state-required curriculum standards for elementary schools include something called "character education" into which teaching tolerance and opposition to genocide will fall. The window of educating "character" opens the possibility of seeing genocide not just in strictly historical terms, but as an aspect of culture. This means that teachers have the potential to be bold in educating about human rights at a young age, and that such legal-moral issues do not need to be left for the university years. All it took was for one visiting 3rd-grader to ask me about who became child soldiers during the Khmer Rouge regime—a question I will never forget—to make me realize that even younger students have the potential for grappling with the same issues that disturb adults.

I think in a way we have been looking at human rights education, under which genocide education falls, as a sort of bell-curve, with the ideal age peaking at undergraduate college age. I would call on us to rethink that graph, and to develop educational models that serve all age levels, child and adult alike.

Of course, more challenging and more central to this discussion is the willingness for large nations and ethnic majorities to take a critical look at their own histories and the consequences of their policies and actions. The United States, for example, has still never taken responsibility for the Native American genocide, nor is it alone in its majoritarian policies that have been responsible for not only genocides throughout history, but cultural genocides that may technically leave the people intact, but destroy their languages, religions, cultures, oral literatures, etc.

Some of the results from our teachers' workshop of March 2006 have proved instructive. After the presentations from the genocide survivors, the group broke out into three smaller groups to address needs and determine next steps. Two of the smaller break-out groups expressed a need for materials and curriculum, including personal stories of genocide and survival, guest speakers, field trips, age-appropriate handouts, teacher training, links to groups such as Facing History and Ourselves already engaged in this kind of tolerance-building work, and books, articles, and films. The third of our three break-out groups spoke more conceptually, defining as the needs "the need to educate ourselves," the need "to make these experiences real for children," and the "need to teach empathy." Suggested methods included nonviolent conflict resolution training; teaching respect for all cultures; creating speakers' bureaus and clearing-houses for curriculum materials; online resource lists and discussion groups; workshops to help child survivors of genocide; work with textbook publishers to include more material on genocide, if not an actual textbook; and "Teach[ing] kids to be activists—connect kids to other kids."

The unanswered questions the teachers had have ranged from the global ("How were refugees received by neighboring countries? How do you find solutions to prevent genocide so it doesn't happen again? How do we build connections between kids who were affected by genocide and those who weren't?

How can we connect the issue of genocide with everyday violence that our kids are facing?") to the more mundane ("How do we build connections across the content areas—science, math, social studies, reading?").

I am also equally convinced that the teaching of history alone, or more accurately, the understanding of genocide as a historical or political phenomenon alone, is not enough. Genocide is also a cultural phenomenon, and anthropology and folklore—the latter of which is especially concerned with human expression—are equally valuable as history in studying and understanding it. Central to the execution of genocidal acts is the spread of a cultural worldview, however temporary or acute, that dehumanizes Others, in what has become known in genocide studies as a ten-stage process (Stanton). This dehumanization typically is encouraged, at least tacitly, by a state actor. The weapons used are a combination of those supplied by larger powers (often with economic support as well) in combination with local weapons, such as machetes and knives. Speaking as a folklorist, it is especially disturbing to me to point out that the mechanism of dehumanization and, later, genocide, is greased by such folkloric genres as stereotype, rumour, and code words and verbal formulas, such as the description of Rwandan Tutsis as "cockroaches" before and during the massacres, and that a further understanding of the workings of negative, destructive folklore needs to be explored. Journalists such as Ravi Agrawal have written about the use of social media in India, especially WhatsApp, as an enabler of this kind of rumour and its relationship to ethnic and religious persecution.

We can talk in our Cambodian Museum, whether giving tours or leading teacher workshops, about the historical factors that led to the rise of the Khmer Rouge. But visitors' questions, the disturbing kind, often revolve around *how* people could have been so morally altered as to be able to carry out such slaughter and cruelty. That "how" is an anthropological question in that it asks what the change was in the social fabric, not just the political-economic circumstances, that would spark violence, destroy the bond of compassion, and obscure remorse. This is a series of questions as true for other genocides as for the Cambodian example. Kaylanee Mam has written on the use of religion and ideology by the Khmer Rouge to promote genocidal practices. Mam, as well as Power, also noted the perversion of family relationships under genocide, whether the deliberate breakdown of family bonds or the use of incest and mutilation to humiliate and further desecrate victims. Showing the anthropological facets—that is, turning a historical exhibit into an ethnographic or ethnohistorical one—requires far more subtlety and complexity than what museum-goers and curators alike are more accustomed to, particularly those unfamiliar with museums as living institutions. And of course it disturbs because the genocide isn't neatly "over" but remains a part of the human animal's capacity for destruction.

I also do not want to neglect the role that oral history documentation can play in the teaching about genocide that continues to take place in our Museum. We undertook in two oral history projects, one, led by anthropology professor Judy Ledgerwood at Northern Illinois University and funded by the Luce Foundation, which deals with life histories, while the other led by me with a local teenage theater company, funded by The History Channel, dealt with the rebuilding of lives and communities in the refugee camps and in Chicago after the years of genocide. One of the deepest silences exists not between Cambodians and Americans, but between some elders and the young generation within the Cambodian-American community. For many families, the issue of survival was not to be spoken about at all (a situation familiar to those who may have worked with European Holocaust survivors). Our oral history training sessions moved some of the young interviewers to ask questions of their parents and grandparents they never broached before. In this sense, genocide education is a component of self-knowledge and self-understanding, and may well become a tool for the children of survivors to better cope with the emotional issues they will face as they deal with the residual trauma, depression, and anger they have been confronted with their whole lives.

In addition to our changing exhibits, the final room on our Museum tour is the Killing Fields Memorial: eighty glass panels etched with names of Cambodian victims, each representing 25,000 victims. If each panel were filled, two million people would be memorialized there. This description, along with details of the systematic torture and execution at S-21, Tuol Sleng Prison, can overwhelm and—for those who haven't been to Cambodia—surprise visitors. The machinery of the European Holocaust is well-known, as is the rapidity of the Rwandan genocide. Our cultural institutions become the vessels for memorializing, educating, and bringing people together, in a safe space across their differences and concerns. Education, memory, the resolution of human conflict, the narrating of history within families and communities, and this primate species' predilection for mass homicide—these are all topics for the practice of anthropology. Moreover, like the Jews, through these museums, the members of the community are able to focus attention on the issues of importance to them. The Cambodians are empowered not only to name genocide and keep the issue and the memory alive, but they are able to use that commemoration to raise other, perhaps difficult topics, such as the provision of health care services to resettled refugees years after resettlement, as well as perhaps the most difficult issue of all—reconciliation, justice for the former Khmer Rouge, and reparations from the U.S. for destruction as a result of the illegal U.S. bombing in the early 1970s.

In 2015 the Museum rededicated itself to its mission, changing the name to the National Cambodian Heritage Museum and adopting as its underlying concept the idea of a "living museum." As explained in a vision statement on its website, which clearly follows from the path the founders set out when it was founded.

> This museum is not a static institution, but an ever-evolving cultural agent where the community members actively take part in making its narratives. The narratives are also shaped through dialogues among Cambodians from different generations, and through dialogues between Cambodians and non-Cambodians. (National Cambodian Heritage Museum 2015)

The significance of this is also that a new generation of younger leaders has taken charge, educators and other professionals in their 30s and 40s, continuing the work begun by the elders in the community. They teach the lessons learned, about genocide, Cambodian culture and history, and Cambodian-American culture and American history. The ideas expressed of agency and narrative demonstrate that museums can no longer be passive but are active participants in education and catalysts even for social change.[2]

A museum is a complex of cultural commons where all these issues—political, historical, cultural, and medical—can be discussed, questioned, hammered out in a way that brings the community toward reconciliation and healing. But the commons doesn't just happen; museum education coupled with folklore and oral history research is the open gate through which this discussion can take place.

NOTES

1. This figure is the subject of debate and numerous articles devoted to this question alone. Estimates range from under 50,000 to 800,000, with the CIA's own estimate in 1980 as 600,000 war-related deaths. How much can be attributed to the bombing is the subject of extensive analysis elsewhere. The larger point is that this war left deep scars on the population even before the Khmer

Rouge took over, and they were initially welcomed as the civil war ended, before anyone knew what their regime would then do.

2. I've written about this more extensively in Westerman 2016, of which this museum was one case study.

Bibliography

Agrawal, Ravi. (2018). *India connected: How the smartphone is transforming the world's largest democracy*. Oxford: Oxford University Press.

Freire, P. (1970). *Pedagogy of the oppressed*, trans. M.B. Ramos. New York: Herder and Herder.

Mam, Kaylanee. (2006). "The endurance of the Cambodian family under the Khmer Rouge regime: An oral history," S.E. Cook, ed., *Genocide in Cambodia and Rwanda: New Perspectives*, pp. 119-62. New Brunswick, N.J.: Transaction Publishers.

Marshall, G.N., T.L. Schell, M.N. Elliott, S.M. Berthold & C. Chun (2005). "Mental health of Cambodian refugees 2 decades after resettlement in the united states," *Journal of the American Medical Association*, 294 (5), 571-79. doi:10.1001/jama.294.5.571

National Cambodian Heritage Museum. (2015). Living museum model. https://www.cambodianmuseum.org/living-model-museum

Power, S. (2002). *'A problem from hell': American and the age of genocide*. New York: Basic Books.

Stanton, G.H. (1996). *The ten stages of genocide*. Genocide Watch. https://www.genocidewatch.com/ten-stages-of-genocide

Westerman, W. (2016). "Museums, refugees, and collaborative social transformation," A.K. Levin, ed., *Global mobilities: Refugees, exiles, and immigrants in museums and archives*, pp. 31-47. New York: Routledge.

Blindness and Banishment in "Rapunzel" and "The Son of Seven Queens"

M. ANJUM KHAN
Avinashilingam Instt. for Home Sc. for Women, Coimbatore

There is past beyond the history. History is a gateway to the past. However, it does not allow one to access everything. In other words, it always falls short of certain truths in the past. As a result, there is a need for counter history and alternative history. This unrecorded history is supplied by folk and mythical literary works. Further, as the original form of folk is oral, it is existing even before the written form of literature. In addition to this, folk is every one's literature. Unlike the written texts which only the literates can read, it can be learnt and taught by everyone.

Another reason is that a folk tale is a literature of the collective voice. In other words, it is the voice of the entire society. It is not just one author who creates the plot, but many who decide the end. In the article titled "A Comparative Study of Folk Tales of UP Tribes and European Fairy Tales," Hasan says, "Narrators often conversed with the audience, modifying the tales to suit the listeners. Listeners, thus, became the co-authors of the stories" (221).

The folk culture of any community or nation holds the key to its evolution and tradition. For instance, the story of "The Thirsty Crow" portrays a clever crow. In India, the crow is considered a bird of importance. It is the vessel for the ancestral spirits on one hand, and on the other, a messenger of visitors. However, in Western folk culture, crow is portrayed as a foolish bird in the story, "Fox and the Crow." Thus, crow is a symbol of tradition and rites in India and not in the West. Likewise, a comparative reading of two different cultures is possible through the reading of their folk and fairy tales.

The folk tales also tell the less told and the untold. One such less told idea is, 'disability.' Disability has evolved with the evolution of mankind. There have been citations of disabled individuals in the ancient texts and classical myths. Irina Metzler traces the social history of disability to the medieval ages in her book, *A Social History of Disability in the Middle Ages: Cultural Considerations of Physical Impairment*. The book is a diachronic discourse of disability in the society. It provides an understanding of the predicament of the disabled individuals. It helps to explore the relationship between the folk tales and the stark reality. In fact, it justifies the reason for the portrayal of disabled characters as social paraya in the folk literature. Metzler categorizes the disabled individuals as liminals:

> I have chosen liminal over marginal, since it better describes the in-between phase that physically impaired people found themselves in, since they are between normatively fixed positions (such as healthy or ill, alive or dead, male or female) rather than completely outside of traditional structures. In this I have followed the previous analysis of liminality derived from anthropological studies, notably in the work of structuralist Victor Turner in the late 1960s on rites of passage. (5)

The literary and non-literary texts have been helpful in excavating the unearthed history of disability. Further, the contextual reading of folk lore and myths has also helped in shifting the historical paradigms. Evidently, there has been abundant scholarship on the subject of disability in the ancient past. There has been revisionist reading of texts and folklores. There have been theories employed to discover the buried and forgotten. David Mitchell and Sharon Snyder observe: "To begin with, a new historicism of disability representations in the humanities sought to perform an anthropological unearthing of images that could help to reconstruct a period's point of view on human variation. Stories provided more than cultural escapism. They situated themselves as explanatory paradigms for revealing the supernatural and social origins of disability's appearance in the world. An early example came in Susan Schoon Eberly's (1988) discussion of the figure of the changeling in European folklore. (200)

A comparative reading of two folk tales representing different cultures in the light of blindness is the key focus of this research essay. The fairy tale, "“Rapunzel" is one of the most liked and widely known European fairy tales. The line, "Rapunzel, Rapunzel, let down your hair, so that I may climb thy golden stair" is like a maxim in the popular culture. It is also known by other titles, like, "Maid in the Tower" and "Tangled." It is one of the Grimm Brothers' fairy tales, first published in 1812. However, it was borrowed by the Grimm Brothers from "Rapunzel" by Friedrich Schulz published in 1790.

The story "Rapunzel" is 'coming of age' version of fairy tale. It is woven with the motif of incarceration and freedom. It is about a beautiful girl with very long tresses and a magically sweet voice. It is about a witch who is adept in spells and charms. It is about a handsome prince who falls in love with a girl of enchanted beauty. In addition to all the explicit themes and motifs, "Rapunzel" has several layers of embedded texts. One such implied theme is 'disability' in general and 'blindness' in particular.

The handsome prince represents blindness in "Rapunzel." It is not that he is a blind individual by birth, but, he becomes one by affliction. He is sentenced to blindness by the witch, Dame Gothel. Perhaps, the impalement of the prince's face on the thorns, is not merely an accident but a wilful charm of Dame Gothel. He is terrified by the presence of an enchantress and the absence of his beloved. He leaps out of the window and is straight away run through by the spikes. As a result, he injures his eyes and becomes blind.

It can be argued that Dame Gothel intends to disable Rapunzel also. When Dame Gothil discovers Rapunzel's secret, she is so furious that she exiles her foster daughter to wilderness. She leaves Rapunzel in wasteland to suffer and become disabled. This is evident when she intimidates the handsome prince with her poetic and metaphorical threat, "she cried mockingly, 'you would fetch your dearest, but the beautiful bird sits no longer singing in the nest; the cat has got it, and will scratch out your eyes as well."

However, the enchantress is not yet content. She wants to avenge her pride and trust. She feels betrayed and defied by both the prince and Rapunzel. She plots to harm the prince and consequently, plants the long ladder of Rapunzel's locks at the window to deceive the prince. She succeeds in her enterprise to bring the downfall of the prince who trespassed on her property. Here, property means both the tall tower and Rapunzel. He has defiled and attained both. She afflicts the prince with blindness which means he is doomed forever.

Blindness is a grave punishment and a severe downfall for the prince. Although, Dame Gothel's foe is a prince but he is reduced to a pauper after losing his sight. He loses all his regal powers. He is abandoned by his own family and subjects. Nobody comes looking for the missing prince. It is implicit that he is become nobody after losing his sight. He lives in wretchedness and despondency, "Then he wandered quite blind about the forest, ate nothing but roots and berries, and did naught but lament and weep over the loss of his dearest wife. Thus he roamed about in misery."

"The Son of Seven Queens" is an Indian folk and fairy tale. It is told in several Indian languages. It has also been translated into English. It is also a part of few folk tale and fairy tale collections. The story is about a son and his seven mothers who are all abandoned by the king. The king is bewitched by a fair enchantress, who as her bride price demands the eyes of the seven queens. The king does not even flinch and blinds all his seven queens and banishes them to a dungeon with their only son. Metaphorically speaking, the king becomes blind and also insane. He is unable to see what he is doing to his family. He is dazzled by the enchanted beauty. He is unable to think for himself and dances to the tune of the enchantress. He loses his reason and sensibility.

The irony in the folk tale "The Son of Seven Queens" is that the king is so charmed by the beauty of the enchantress that he blinds all his seven wives. He is blinder than his seven queens. What is more, the seven victims of the king are his own wives, the queens. He is unable to see reason after gazing at the enchanted beauty. Unlike the king, the seven queens were able to see beyond what bare eyes can see. They are able to foresee the future. They are able to see the lurking danger and warn the king, 'Now the King was very fond of hunting, and one day, before he started, the seven Queens sent him a message saying, "May it please our dearest lord not to hunt towards the north to-day, for we have dreamt bad dreams, and fear lest evil should befall you."'

Another point for reflection is that the Enchantress orders only the king to bring her the eyes of the seven queens. She does not ask him to imprison them in the dungeon. It is of his own accord that the king decides to banish the blinded queens to the dungeon. He discards his queens like old dolls, "The King was so carried away by the glamour of the white hind's magical beauty, that he went home at once, had the eyes of his seven Queens taken out, and, after throwing the poor blind creatures into a noisome dungeon whence they could not escape, set off once more for the hovel in the ravine; bearing with him his horrible offering." It is because the blinded queens are of no value or use to him. Further, he does not want them to escape their blindness.

In fact, the king does not even want the seven queens to live any further. He does not provide any food or care for the blind queens. It is their son who brings them some food to survive. Soon after the son begins to walk, he becomes the bread-winner for his ill-fated family, "Almost as soon as he could walk about he began scraping at the mud wall of their dungeon, and in an incredibly short space of time had made a hole big enough for him to crawl through. Through this he disappeared, returning in an hour or so laden with sweetmeats, which he divided equally amongst the seven blind Queens."

It can be concluded that blindness nullifies even the social position of the blind individual. The seven queens who lived in such glory are doomed to abyss. The worst happens only after they lose the ability to see. Before the queens are blinded, they lead a luxurious and pleasant life. The king adores and waits upon his seven queens, "Meanwhile the seven Queens lived luxuriously in a splendid palace, attended by hundreds of female slaves, and fed to their hearts' content on sweetmeats and confectionery." Similarly, in the fairy tale, "Rapunzel," the prince loses all his regal powers and riches after becoming blind. It disables him completely. He is unable to return to his family or lead a decent life.

A comparative reading of "Rapunzel" and "The Son of Seven Queens" divulges, more or less, similar social conditions of the blind individuals. In both tales, the blind individuals are banished, uncared for, and beyond self-reliance. They seek some miracle to cure them. The prince is cured by the magical tears of Rapunzel and the son miraculously restores the eyes of his seven mothers. In both the tales, blindness is followed by abject despair, hopelessness, and desolation.

Nonetheless, there are also subtleties in the treatment of blindness in the two different societies. For instance, in "Rapunzel," the prince is abandoned by his family. Nobody comes looking for him. However in "The Son of Seven Queens," the son does not leave the side of his seven blind mothers. He could have left them and found a better life for himself, but he does not do that. This subtlety is evident even in today's scenario. Jan Grue surveys, "US Disability Studies conceptualizes disabled people as an ethnic-cultural minority, UK Disability Studies conceptualizes disabled people as an oppressed class, and Scandinavian Disability Studies conceptualizes disabled people as the beneficiaries of welfare state programmes and interventions" (30).

Undoubtedly, the folk tales which are part of the collective conscience of larger cultures and society cannot be dismissed. They constitute the counter histories and tell the untold. Maria Nikolajeva quotes Jack Zipes, "literature is inseparable from the society within which it is created" (187). An Indian scholar, G.N. Kama writes about disability in India. He documents the history of disability in Indian society. He also cites from Indian ancient texts revealing the social condition of disabled individuals. He cites from Manu, "Manu, however, does not seem inclined to assign the disabled an equal status in society" (60).

The society as whole has a vital role to play in the change of attitude and values. In the past, it loathed and banished disability. In present, the society condescends and marginalizes the same. It is the society which makes a woman 'a woman' and a disabled 'a disabled.' Rebecca Raphael remarks, "The body has not changed, but the social environment has. Impairment becomes disability because of the ways society chooses to build its spaces and communicate its information" (3).

The folk and fairy tales saturated in culture and tradition provide history and morality. The poetic justice rendered at the end of the stories offers a sense of moral security and fairness. This helps in reinforcing the codes of integrated living. The advocacy for disability is the need of the hour. Dan Goodley quotes Karl Marx, "Disability affects us all, transcending class, nation and wealth. The notion of the TAB—Temporarily Able Bodied—recognizes that many people will at some point become disabled" (2).

Works Cited

Brothers, Grimm. *The Project Gutenberg EBook of Grimms' Fairy Tales*, trans. Edgar Taylor and Marian Edwardes. 2008.

Goodley, Dan. *Disability Studies: An Interdisciplinary Introduction*. New Delhi: Sage, 2011.

Grue, Jan. *Disability and Discourse Analysis*. Burlington: Ashgate, 2015.

Hasan, Seemin. "A Comparative Study of Folk Tales of UP Tribes and European Fairy Tales," *Indian Literature*, Vol. 53, No. 2 (250) (March/ April 2009), pp. 202-8.

"Indian Fairy Tales: The Son of Seven Queens." *Sacred Text*. http://www.sacred-texts.com/hin/ift/ift17.htm

Kama, G.N. *Disability Studies in India: Retrospects and Prospects*. New Delhi: Gyan, 2001.

Metzler, Irina. *A Social History of Disability in the Middle Ages: Cultural Considerations of Physical Impairment*. New York: Routledge, 2013.

Mitchell, David L. and Sharon L. Snyder. "Representation and Its Discontents: The Uneasy Home of Disability in Literature and Film." *Handbook of Disability Studies*, ed. Gary L. Albrecht, Katherine Seelman and Michael Bury. New Delhi: Sage, 2001.

Nikolajeva, Maria. "Marvels & Tales" *Journal of Fairy-Tale Studies*, Vol. 16, No. 2 (2002), pp. 171-87.

Raphael, Rebecca. *Biblical Corpora: Representation of Disability in Hebrew Biblical Literature*. New York: Continuum, 2008.

Rewriting Folk Narratives: A Case Study of Canadian Feminist Fantastical Voices

SUMITA PURI
Dyal Singh Evening College, University of Delhi

The paper is an attempt to look at myths, fairy tales and fables which have originally been a representation of patriarchal world with women characters delineated not only as subordinate to man but also as incapable of living a life of their own without being dependent on man physically, emotionally and socially carrying the image of a weak and docile species. This stereotypical picture of woman in social and cultural representation has remained unchanged in many forms of folk narratives in patriarchal society. Children especially girls have been indoctrinated by this treatment of women as second sex, that is, man's other. Outwardly such stories and tales are entertaining but inwardly they have deeply ingrained social values patriarchy has grossly implanted for the exploitation of women. Subjection of women to their physical, sexual bondage unable to claim an independent identity of their own in a world structured on sexual binarism due to patriarchal domination and marginalization of women has been subverted by some Canadian feminist writers by rewriting the traditionally known myths, fairy tales and fables to remove the negative role of women in an effort to prove that women are by no means inferior to man. This way, children will have to be nurtured from the young age that women have potential on a par with man thus challenging the heterosexual dependency syndrome.

In the past it was a common practice in almost all societies to tell folktales and fairy tales especially to children, and such tales had far reaching impact on the minds of children. Children enjoy listening to stories and when they grow up such stories heard long ago bear meaningful interpretations of life and give powerful lessons, moral values and wisdom. But the appeal of folk narratives irrespective of age and race is universal. In this regard what Linda Dégh writes is very true: "Narration is ageless. The impulse to tell a story and the need to listen to it have made narrative the natural companion of man throughout the history of civilization. Stories are able to adapt themselves to any local and social climate. They are old and venerable, but they are also new and up to date" (1972: 53). Bruno Bettelheim, in an attempt to comprehend the significance of myths, fairy tales, and folktales, writes:

> When all the child's wishful thinking gets embodied in a good fairy; all his destructive wishes in an evil witch; all his fears in a voracious wolf; all the demands of his conscience in a wise man encountered on an adventure; all his jealous anger in some animal that picks out the eyes of his archrivals—then the child can finally begin to sort out his contradictory tendencies. Once this starts, the child will be less and less engulfed by unmanageable chaos. (66)

In many societies fairy tales, folktales, more especially and myths, less commonly became popular texts to fulfill the pedagogic needs for children. Bettelheim further observes, "fairytales teach little about the specific conditions of life in modern mass society; these tales were created long before .... But more can be learned from them about the inner problems of human beings, and of the right solutions to their predicaments in any society, than from any other type of story within a child's comprehension" (*ibid.* 5). Of the other genres of folk literature, children are very fond of fables may be mentioned. A fable normally contains animals—monkeys, wolfs, bears, crocodiles, birds, and so on wrought with human emotions and conflicts. The child extrapolates that the animals speak, feel and understand with it, and through the animals' experience, gains knowledge for himself/

herself. The manifold aspects of an individual's personality are discerned through the reading of fables. The fable is marked by the fabulous; the characters are embodied with human attributes undergoing trials and tribulations. The animals in the fables guide heroes through forests, aid in rescuing captives, mermaids fall in love with humans, frogs turn into princes, the pussy cat and the fox are stereotyped as being wily and cunning respectively. Fables state a moral truth, "demand and threaten—they are moralistic—or they just entertain" (*ibid.* 27)

On the other hand, folk and fairy tales provide a plethora of adventures, encounters, and vicissitudes for children towards facing the real world while serving as source of enhancing knowledge and giving enjoyment. The multiple ends of fairy tales are given here:

> Fairy tales, unlike any other form of literature, direct the child to discover his identity and calling, and they also suggest what experiences are needed to develop his character further. Fairy tales intimate that a rewarding, good life is within one's reach despite adversity—but only if one does not shy away from the hazardous struggles without which one can never achieve true identity. These stories promise that if a child dares to engage in this fearsome and taxing search, benevolent powers will come to his aid, and he will succeed. The stories also warn that those who are too timorous down to a humdrum existence—if an even worse fate does not befall them. (Bettelheim 24)

Myths, on the other hand, are sacred and considered to have happened in the hoary past even before the birth of man and other living beings, and a source of rites and religion of a nation or a people. Adam, Eve, Brahma, Vishnu, Siva, Rama and Krishna are mythical characters. Such stories are on a different plane in their respective cultures. Fairy tales and folktales are aimed as the stepping stones for laying the foundation for the personality of the individual. They are the social and cultural signifiers embedded in the narratives to be conveyed to the society. Scientific study of fairy tales, folktales and myths have been done by anthropologists, ethnologists, folklorists, linguists, literary scholars for the discovery and reinterpretation of their concealed meanings. The question that arises is, that are these stories, simply an exportation into the realm of fantasy so as to reflect reality? Through the centuries, fairy tales and fables have been read as a part of children's literature but have formed an important impact on the psychology of adults as well. Western traditional fairy tales have served the precise purpose of transferring cultural values, social codes and mannerisms to people for generations. But what are these social and cultural norms? Are they not the integral essentials of the family system in which we are born and brought up; the patriarchal hegemonic set-up in which we grow up; the society that tutors that the father is the head of the family. Is it not further that since the financial power lies in the hands of the father, he is entitled to lay down the rules and the code of conduct in the family making the mother and the children dependent on him financially as well as emotionally. In many cultural representations we find the commodification and inferiorization of women and children. For instance, marriage is in the form of transaction, selling and buying. So, it is a transaction of money and phallic power between two men and never between women. Women are objects of male desire who pass from one man to another and relapse into the system and Luce Irigaray reads this relapse as a penalty. The woman of the house becomes subordinate; she is labelled as the 'inferior sex.' She is confined to her domestic space performing her household chores with humility and dexterity. She learns submission and servility towards the bread earner of the family. She is the Annapurna and ought to cook delicious food, produce and rear children perfecting the art with compliance. When she is young, she imbibes gender stereotypes of obedience, self-abnegation and obsequiousness. The performance of the ascribed role is carried out throughout lifetime as daughter, wife and mother.

The coercive forces of patriarchy resulting in the domination and abuse of women have formed the subject matter of women's literature time and again. Female writers have accentuated the marginalization of the so-called 'weaker sex' in their literature. Writers either posited the state of women but left things unsaid or utilized their writing as a potent tool to express the pent up anger against this oppression. In the twentieth century, women writers took up the task of "phallic criticism," as Mary Ellman puts it, to expose the sexist criticism in literature. They decided to write—to write stories in which women seek their individuality. Shirin Kudchedkar writes in "Feminist Voices from India and Canada": "Western feminist writers (and Western has hitherto meant White Canadian, American or European writers) are concerned with a woman's or girl's encounter with the world, her efforts to define herself, to find viable ways of living." (2)

Oral narratives in many cultures have served as a medium to transmit social and cultural values, beliefs, traditions, customs, while at the same time they are a source of entertainment. However, when they are seen from the feminist point of view they will certainly represent gendered discourse in which one will find the explicit sexism, the patriarchal voice suppressing women. Feminist movement in Canada aims at exposing the politics of the clichéd projections of women in literature and culture. They revisit the representation of women in folktales and fairy tales, analyzing how these narratives have depicted women as the timid object of male gaze and the consequential transmission of the dominant power structures of patriarchy. Traditional tales have been operational in setting these cultural constructs directly or vicariously. Through them patriarchal programming is done and social values as deemed fit are indoctrinated by patriarchy so that women essentially perpetuate these norms and values of social constructs with acquiescence. Women in folk narratives are marked for their beauty, youth and innocence. They are the passive maidens who have no will of their own and are incapable of thinking rationally for themselves. The narratives project them as inferior to men and having accepted patriarchal hegemony. In her efforts at defining the role of women in tales and the subsequent effects on the readers, Kaarina Kailo tells us that women are shown as the meek sisters who serve as hand-maidens to men, from dwarves to princes; they are young princesses waiting earnestly for their princes, savior and lord to come and rescue them from the clutches of the diabolical beasts. The male heroes or princes derive pleasure in gazing at their female object of desire and conquering them and thereby satisfying their ego. In her words:

> Even when women seemingly occupy centrestage as the main characters of Western fairy tales, these stories simply reproduce Christian, mainstream, patriarchal fantasies about proper female behaviour. The typical polarized models of femininity that girls end up internalizing as the good/bad gender-specific modes of behaviour are equally empowering for them. Folktale "heroines" . . . remain locked in their need for protection, rescue and romanticized heterosexual dependency. (87)

Feminist writers in Canada have therefore taken up the task of retelling these tales to assert their vision of a land of promised equality. Kaarina Kailo points out that rewriting fairy tales and myths help women writers: "to interact with . . . internalized images of femininity and to play-act with characters in . . . [their] inner theatre," and it is their duty "to go through these stages of deconstruction (taking our traditions and cultures apart so as to see what makes them tick) and the stage of reconstructions, re-visioning, re-appropriation" (91).

The project of rewriting the established tales begins with the prime myth—the myth of creation. The Fall of Man or the original sin has been religiously attributed to Eve. According to Genesis, the biblical story of creation, Lilith, the prototype of Eve was created before Eve as man's equal. When she was denied her sexual authority she fled in quest of her freedom. Hence, Lilith is mythicized culturally as a sexual she-beast who is untamed and whose sexuality is unveiled for all to glare at. God then created Eve as subordinate to Adam/Man and the former tasted the forbidden fruit succumbing to Satan's temptations. The biblical story renders Eve as a seductive temptress whose association with the serpent led to the cognizance of her sexuality and brought anarchy to man's blissful state. So culture mythifies man as the innocent victim and the woman as the seductress. Woman's sexuality is thus linked to Satan—the originator of evil in the world. Hence, her sexuality must be repressed and not given a chance to unleash or else she would become bestial and uncontrollable like Lilith. For this reason, man needs to maintain that whenever a woman expresses her sexual desires she is actually exhibiting masculine traits since sexuality is his tool of power. Her sexual assertion can only bring chaos to mankind so she needs to be submissive, subdued and compliant for the betterment of the entire human race. Hence, all of Eve's daughters, who have asserted their sexuality, have been characterized as dangerous. In the words of Tamara Steinborn: "A close analysis of our culture shows how the true daughters of Eve, all womankind, have been myth-laden to a negative extreme. . . . Woman, as virago, has become dangerous, overpowering, and sexually threatening to man in his world of reason and order" (35). Milton describes the classical image of Eve:

> Eve: "But to Adam in what sort
> Shall I appear? ...
> But keep the odds of Knowledge in my power
> in Female Sex, the more to draw his love,
> and render me more equal, and perhaps
> a thing not undesirable. (*Paradise Lost*)

The text clearly typifies that the evil in Eve or woman is closely associated with her sexuality. In order to de-mythify the archetypal image of Eve, Virginia Lee Hines presents two different interpretations of the 'Eve' story in her poem "An Old Story". In its first section, the poet describes how Eve, "Motherless," became the mother of all the women on Earth, and thus, initiated her daughters into sin—the sin of the expression of their sexual urges. Eve's original behaviour in the garden became the "thorny grove" for all women. She imbued women with their feminine body parts, "certain breasts, womb soft skin," along with a craving to break free from the clutches of repressed sexuality. She writes:

> Oh, I feel now
> how she felt confined to Eden, naked,
> so innocent longing for sin.
> Let me set down my cup of cocoa,
> grab my coat, my purse,
> run from ordered house,
> take chances in unknown territory. (See Hines 33-34)

In the second part of the poem, Eve is emblematic of the modern woman caught in the web of penury, "cooking oatmeal mornings on an undependable gas burner" with no one to count on in an urban materialistic world, ever struggling for survival and identity. Instead of showing Eve lurking in the dark shadows of lust and eroticism, it is Adam, with his "brash craziness" and "uncertain temperament" that encroaches upon her world. Adam yearns to fulfill his carnal appetite and ego by conquering her in the sexual act:

> intrudes
> into my wanderings, calling my name.
> He lusts for me, the reluctant
> twin. We roll into each other
> bruising our skins, our egos,
> then fly apart.

Eve's or the woman's body succumbs to male passion and the original garden turns her body into a garden where Adam wanders in to pluck her whenever he wills to do so:

her body yielding to passion, birth—
woman becomes a garden.

Virginia Lee Hines, thus, breaks the traditional notion of Eve as the original enchantress along with her daughters as evil or the 'mad women in the attic' to borrow Sandra Gilbert and Susan Gubar's phraseology. The retelling of the myth articulates the silenced—the plight of women as objects of male gaze and erotic desire.

In a similar vein in the designated conventional fairy tales the plots consists of a young prince falling in love with a poor girl followed by their marriage as consummation of their love. So the poor girl gets to marry a rich handsome prince, after ordeals and tribulations, perhaps involving repeated transformations, and thereafter lives happily ever after. The young girl is illustrated as a paragon of beauty, innocence, docility and femininity. The prince ought to be the brave gallant riding on horses, fighting dragons and monsters, and, in short, the epitome of masculinity. However, in many fairy tales the oppressed heroine undergoes extremes of torture and suffering and fights to defeat the evil villains with which she reunites the prince. Such is the case with the heroine of Cinderella tale type.

What happened after the prince married Cinderella? Elizabeth Greene? gives us a sequel to the tale in a different tone and a not so happy ending. Greene's fairy tale, "Cinderella's Daughters" does not begin conventionally 'once upon a time.' It opens fifteen or twenty years after the marriage of Cinderella with her prince. The original fairy tale heroine has not altered a bit. She is the same Cinderella, who was "sweet and good in the face of the wicked stepmother and stepsisters" (See Greene 60-65), likes romances and picture books, and "only cared about running the house and taking care of people and gardens and helping the poor." However, in Greene's narrative, Cinderella's daughters Annabelinda and Zoe, who were lovely and intellectual when they were born, do not turn into the typecast heroines. The first disappointment comes when the reader is told that they are not beautiful. Annabelinda has sallow thin shoulders and Zoe is overweight with bad skin. When they play house, they cook stories of "bloodcurdling adventures and escapes." In place of boys, it is the female dolls who slay the dragons and rescue others. In total, defiance of the cultural norms, the girls are rude and moody and "unprincess like" who prefer to stay gloomy and morose rather than being cheerful and bright in public. To the mother's amazement, Annabelinda reads historical novels at the age of ten while Zoe reads poetry which her mother fails to understand. The sisters even discuss their bodies, desires and embarrassments furtively. Annabelinda has only girlfriends and Zoe goes out only with boys. The former writes refined film and play reviews while the latter produces luxuriant poems and spiteful journals. Cinderella's agony is described as: "Cinderella began to get headaches and bad bouts of bronchitis. . . . Her daughters should be growing into beauty, but every day took them further from feminine perfection. What prince would look at them? How would they make their way in the world? How would they find happy endings?"

The twist in this story, as in the original one, comes with the entry of the fairy godmother. The prince invites the fairy godmother to come and stay with them to restore the chaotic order. Cinderella's agony is put to rest as the fairy godmother tells the sisters: "you are each the heroines of your own lives, and you will find your own transformations. Your mother will understand that."

The reader may expect that the godmother is successful in transforming the sisters who eventually meet their princes, get married, and live happily ever after. But the author has a different story to tell. For Annabelinda "heterosexual romantic love remained a closed book," and "she did meet a woman she loved." She begins to teach and write, and in time, becomes a renowned feminist. Because of having an archetype for a mother, she tries "not to write too harshly of women who made conventional choices." Greene depicts Zoe's fate as: "Zoe herself, torn between example of mother and sister, went to graduate school, got a job, fell in love, got pregnant, miscarried, married and had children in that order. She couldn't help being grateful for her husband's affections, and the power shifted in their relationship so that she was always trying to please him and he was always asking for more"

Zoe finally ends her marriage and recuperates the wounds of an unhappy wedded life. She takes care of her children, falls in love again, but does not marry again. She begins to write meaningful poetry and becomes a successful writer too. Cinderella accepts her daughters' choices gradually and adores her successive generations.

Elizabeth Greene's reshaping of the Cinderella story problematizes the objectification of women and the need to change the accepted patterns of dominant patriarchy. In Greene's fairy tale men do not have much role to play. The prince has no masculine prowess to display; the daughters do not meet their princes. The female protagonists challenge the sweet, pretty, submissive stereotype. The fairy godmother does not advise the girls to follow the conventions. The sister who makes the conformist choice ends up with a broken marriage and bruised heart. It is only when the two sisters resolve to live and grow independently that the author finally provides them with a happy ending. Greene closes the narrative with the words: "There are other stories of Cinderella's daughters. Probably you know some yourself. But these are the two I choose to tell."

In order to present how women have been 'pickled' for the male gaze, Kaarina Kailo re-interprets the fairy tale of "The Snow White". Like Cinderella, the Snow White also incorporates the myth of the beautiful princess craving for the "waited-for-prince." She is as white as snow, who needs to starve herself in a coffin, to stay "eternally young, skinny, beautiful, desirable, rescue-worthy." (Kailo 89) She is the ideal woman, perfect in beauty and worth, 'pickled' and 'preserved' for the male gaze of the prince who will kiss her to make her immortal. Kailo's student, Caroline Desbiens-Magalios, expresses the Snow White syndrome as: "Snow White is the ideal woman once preserved under the glass coffin: passive, virginal, sublimely beautiful and deliciously sensual, like the forbidden fruit. She becomes the apple herself which the prince will pick and taste without fear of punishment, for the standard is different: arousal of the erotic power constitutes a woman's fall but a man's elevation." (*Ibid.*)

Similarly "Red Riding Hood" is also associated with the propagation of females with a sexual passivity and dependence on men. The Little Red Riding Hood has to deliver some delicacies to her grandmother who stays in a cottage in the forest. Her mother forbids her not to go through the woods and to take the longer route fearing the wolf could devour the little girl. The Red Riding Hood promises to obey her mother but gets tempted to take the short cut through the woods. The wolf however notices her and eats both the Red Riding Hood and her grandmother eventually.

In "Re-viewing the Life and Times of Little Red Riding Hood," Gretchen Sankey explains that the story is not just a simple fairy tale, but an attempt at the dissemination of the tenets of sexual passivity and self-abnegation in women. The wolf in the story is the "predatorial man, inclined to seduce if given the slightest chance." (Sankey 53)

The mother prohibits the Riding Hood from going into the woods for fear of the wolf who would ravish her. The Red Riding Hood's decision to explore the forbidden territories is equated with her violent sexual emotions, also associated with her red cap, the colour red being associated with danger as well as passion. Since the little girl gives in to her innocuous desires, she has to pay the price and has to bear the burden of guilt of the sexual abuse for having chosen the unsafe route herself. The fairy tale distinctly admonishes little girls from defying the said norms. Jack Zipes disputes that the writers of fairy tales "were men who were interested in preserving patriarchal norms, and therefore, Little Red Riding Hood's image must be seen as a male creation and projection," and that the widespread and friendly reception of the fairy tale owes to the "general acceptance of the cultural notions of sexuality, sex roles and domination embedded in it." (Qtd. Sankey 54)

Another of the 'pickled' heroines in fairy tales is "The Little Mermaid." The Little Mermaid is the loveliest and prettiest of all her sisters. The story tells us: "all the Mer-princesses were extremely beautiful, but the little mermaid, who was the youngest, had the prettiest hair . . . and the bluest eyes." (Grimm 191) The little mermaid is not allowed to leave the coral palace and swim freely in the blue sea as per the Mer-king's law. However, when she turns fifteen, she is permitted to go above the sea where she rescues a handsome prince from drowning in the storm and falls in love with him. In order to win his love, she appeals to the sea-witch to get rid of her tail and have a pair of legs in its place. The witch agrees to do so in exchange of the mermaid's melodious voice. The mermaid turns speechless and goes to the prince's palace but is not fortunate enough to get reciprocation of her love and so finally retreats.

What is the message of this fairy tale? At first, the little mermaid is forbidden to violate or question her father's law. Being a clichéd fairy tale female protagonist, her only aim is to win the prince's love and get married to him. Kaarina Kailo elucidates: "True to this fixated frozen image, girls are conditioned with the dominant fairy tales in the Western hemisphere to pickle themselves, to repress their orality, to hold their tongues and to internalize the sexual dogmas uncritically. The Little Mermaid is the arch representative of the woman who is willing to give up speech, self-expression, language in order to 'get' her prince." (Kailo 88) Such models of self-effacement are abundantly prevalent in Western fairy tales to propagate the Christian concepts of self-sacrifice and humility in women. The only fulfillment a woman can seek is in finding her companion, who will aid her in reaching her womanhood, give birth to his children and live happily ever after.

Pauline Rankin reworks the Mermaid tale in her story titled "A Mermaid Tail." The author opens her narrative with the declaration: "THIS IS NO WIDE-EYED cartoon story," emphatically stating that the reader must not expect it to be the usual fairy tale. The Little Mermaid of this story is a powerful and determined swimmer who swims through murkier waters, strange places and colder seas to look for her companion. There is no Mer-king and no forbidden law to establish the negation of patriarchy and its edicts straightaway. Outside the realm of the patriarchal structure, the mermaid is free to swim above the seas and explore the unfamiliar territories. The mermaid finally reaches a land house where, instead of meeting her prince, she meets a woman: "There she saw the most beautiful woman walking along the shore, on sturdy and powerful legs. The mermaid hauled herself out of the water, where she lay half fainting with exertion and delight. The land-woman hurried to her side. . . . She almost fainted with delight, as well." (See Rankin 42-43)

The mermaid and the land-woman begin to visit each other frequently—one day on the land and the other day on the sea. The two gradually fall in love with each other and make love to each other. In opposition to the original mermaid story, the mermaid does not have to forfeit her tail or voice for gaining the love of her companion. The author writes: "the land-woman spoke in human tones. The mermaid sounded her dolphin voice. They did not miss the words."

In a male-governed story, the mermaid loses her identity fully. Earlier, it is the father who lays down the rules and later, it is the prince whose love forces her to forego her selfhood. Once she is out of this domination, she is free to choose her partner, who need not be a man anymore. Neither of the two women needs to sacrifice her individuality. The mermaid feels that she does not want to give up her potent swimming tail and the land-woman wishes not to lose her strong legs. The writer renders a solution: "they decided to continue as they were: sometimes in land, sometimes in water." In this manner, the duo stayed together by lending each other enough space for themselves, which is denied in patriarchy. In the re-writing of the tale, Pauline Rankin, therefore, brings to light the repression of women and offers the reader an alternative matriarchal society in which women need not deprive themselves of their emotional or sexual desires. There is complete absence of male characters in the story to authenticate the feminist writer's assertion that women's happiness does not necessarily lay with heterosexuality in addition to the fact that lesbian relations are equally promising. Noted lesbian feminist critics Alice, Gordon, Debbie and Mary underscore this point: "[L]esbians, by loving women and not men, pose a direct threat to the very basis of male supremacy. From this analysis, we conclude that lesbians have the ability and commitment to women that will be necessary to overthrow male supremacy and its attendant forms of oppression." (Qtd. Andermahr 134)

The male sovereignty is also endorsed in the famous "Rapunzel"—a tale of a couple who steal a handful of rampion from a witch's garden and have to pay the price by giving their loveable daughter, Rapunzel, to the witch. Rapunzel is locked in a castle and is forbidden to step outside. Whenever the witch has to climb the tower to reach Rapunzel's room she utters: "Rapunzel, Rapunzel, let down your golden hair" and uses her long thick tresses as a ladder. One day, a prince riding by hears Rapunzel's melodious voice and gets enchanted by it. He gets to know the witch's secret and cries: "Rapunzel, Rapunzel, let down your golden hair." He uses her hair as a staircase to reach the top. The young girl feels that the prince would love her more and plans to escape with him. The narrative that follows is the witch's finding out their plan of elopement, planting Rapunzel in a remote desert, the prince turning blind followed by meeting his beloved finally, getting his eyesight back and their staying happy ever after. At the outset, the fairy tale is a regular story of a prince rescuing a young girl entrapped by a wicked witch. Nonetheless, one cannot ignore the gendered values embedded in it. The tale, once again, exemplifies women as compliant and cowardly waiting for their princes to come and rescue them. 'Pickled' and 'Preserved' for the prince to come, Rapunzel sings in her solitude and is dumb to the extent of not ever planning to escape herself. The account reports that the protagonist had never seen a man in her life and yet she feels that she would be happier with the prince and not the witch! Such stories and such heroines are consciously constructed for the sustentation of the patriarchal order that validates the fact that only a man can provide physical as well as emotional security to a woman. The female protagonist carries the cultural paradigms of beauty and dependency while the male protagonist conveys the virtues of valour and independence. Kaarina Kailo points out once again in this respect: "girls are encouraged to put the lid on their self-development, while life is an open field, an open season for the self-expanding boys," (Kailo 89) so true, in the case of Rapunzel.

A twist of perception is palpable in the Rapunzel story in Melissa Branicky's poem "Rapunzel, Rapunzel, let down your hair. . . ." The poem offers a substitute to the young damsel who gets lured by the prince in hope of fulfillment of emotional and sexual desires. Like Rapunzel, every woman gives in to her desires and lets down her hair. Like the prince, every man uses a woman's beauty as a staircase to reach the top. He entices her by praising her looks but his real motive is to satisfy his physical needs only. The poet writes:

> Like Rapunzel,
> every time a man calls out to you,
> you throw him down

your long thick hair,
slowly each of them has climbed,
groping his way up your back,
tangling your beauty into a ladder. (See Melissa Branicky 50-51)

Slowly, the man empowers the woman completely on the pretext of making love to her. The woman's body begins an ache but she is acquiescent with the illusion that the man is fulfilling her needs:

All the while
Your neck strains,
the flesh itching
with the ache
you constantly mistake for desire.

The poet pleads to Rapunzel and all the women to understand that the man in her life is no prince but an ordinary mortal who hurts her physically and mentally by displaying his superiority over her in the sexual act and otherwise. Each time Rapunzel is wounded she comes to the aid of the poet to recuperate:

So you come to me,
And I kiss your bruises,
But I can never make you realize,
He has yet to be a prince.

The poet offers an alternative to Rapunzel—to cut her hair permanently so that no prince can injure by climbing over her. The poet, thus, advises women to break free from heteronormative bondage and to further seek alternative modes of happiness:

Let me wield my shears
and free you from these burdens.
I can no longer bear to watch you
Supporting this kind of weight.

Canadian feminist writers have also focused on short fables and stories to strengthen the vision of a utopian land where women will enjoy the same rights and privileges as men do. In order to illustrate this one can look at "Plucking" by Lorna Schwenk and "Tree and Bear" by Frances Rooney. The formal fable demonstrates the woman's agony of being used and discarded emotionally and physically by the man. "Plucking" is the story of two birds of opposite sexes and the various stages of their relationship. The narrative unfolds with the she-bird entering the life of the he-bird who is stupefied by the former's looks. The he-bird next seeks permission to pluck one of her feathers. The courtship begins and the female bird blossoms in love. The wooing ceases but the he-bird continues to pluck more of her feathers without even asking her. The she-bird begins to wither as her feathers are plucked and splotches of white skin begin to appear: "The plucking continued, however, late at night when she was defenceless and tired, or at a weak moment when she needed him the most" (See Schwenk 31-32). The plucking further continued till one day she realized that not a single feather was left on her body: "she was completely bare. Not a feather left. Nothing. She was a bald, pale, naked, embarrassed bird. Didn't even *look* a bird anymore."

The she-bird searches her house for her feathers and finds some in his ashtray, some in the dust, some caked and dried, and some in the basement with worn socks and broken shoes. The bird is hurt at finding out how her feathers had been used by her companion. The story ends with the bird's realization that she has been exploited by him and she has to wait for her feathers to grow back on her body. And the author tells us, that each time, it took a long time to heal her wounds, indicating that it was an ongoing process: "He called her later that day to say he didn't need her anymore, so she went off to recuperate and wait for her feathers to grow back, but it took a long time. It always did."

Symbolically, a bird is associated with freedom and flight yet the writer portrays the bird as helpless and clinging to the opposite sex for support in order to bring out the irony. Plucking, therefore, serves her as a metaphor for the sexual exploitation of the female sex and the loss of feathers signifies her loss of identity. The writer does not state the moral but leaves it for the reader to interpret. She implicitly hints that women unknowingly submit to men as the system coerces them to do so. The writer, through the fable, raises her voice against this sexual oppression with an advice for women to desist from heterosexual enslavement.

If Lorna Schwenk registers her protest vicariously, Frances Rooney tells a fabulous tale where the feminist writer's claim is apparent. "Tree and Bear" is situated in a verdant forest where the flora and fauna coexist happily. A curse befalls the forest due to which there is complete destruction. All the living creatures perish and when light is restored after a period of complete darkness, no life is left, except in a half-grown sapling. The soil in which the little Tree stood is poisonous and so the poor Tree awaits her death. When the Tree opens her eyes, she sees that a small Bear is clinging onto her trunk. The Bear tells her that everything has been devastated and that they should leave the place at once. The Tree believes that this is not possible and tells the Bear: "I can't. I can't move. This is where I started to grow, and if I cannot grow here, I must die here. That is the law for Trees. . . . I am dead already. I just don't know it yet because there are still leaves on my branches, and my bark has not turned to charcoal. My life is over, Bear. That is hard, but it is true." (See Rooney 33-37)

The Bear tries hard to persuade the Tree but to no avail. The Tree advocates that if she endeavours to uproot herself she would get hurt and bruised, for no Tree has ever dared to take such a step! Trees are supposed to grow and die at their fixed places. The Tree says: "no Tree has ever walked in the whole back time of earth. Never, never, never, it can't be done." The spirit of Hope reads the Tree's mind and appears in order to impart some of her 'self' to the Tree. She assures the Tree that although it is extremely difficult to relocate oneself, yet struggling to live is more promising than waiting to die. Hope comforts the Tree: "Your heart will not break, dear Tree. It has broken already. Now it is healing. The pain you feel is the pain of life, of being alive, of becoming and growing strong, and seeing what you must do, and being afraid, and not holding back in fear. Your heart will not break again, Tree, not the way it has. It will never again feel the pain it has felt. That I promise you, Tree."

The Tree agrees to accompany the Bear and with great effort and pain pulls her roots out of the earth. Her branch breaks and her back is torn, yet with Hope in heart she advances with the Bear. The Bear kisses her roots and throughout the night aids her in learning to walk. Both of them become strong and happy towards their journey: "towards other animals for Bear to run with, toward other Trees for Tree to intertwine her branches with, and toward rich and nourishing soil to feed Tree's bruised roots and trunk and branches and leaves."

The Tree in the fable connotes the woman who has lost everything on account of some tragedy and does not have the courage to stand in the face of adversity. The fact that women have been tutored since childhood to be reliant on their fathers and husbands makes them so vulnerable that they begin to believe that moving out of their confined space is next to impossible—the law for trees as the story tells us. Women do have a choice: either they can remain in their defined roles and suffer and die or strive towards a better life even if that is only possible at the cost of defying the patriarchal norms. The Bear becomes the spokesperson of the writer, who lends to the reader, the moral of the fable: "Tree, I know it's impossible. I know it's never been done. I know you can't. . . . You can either stay here or do what's ordinary and tree-like and possible, or you can do the extraordinary and the impossible and leave here. You can stay and die, or you can go and live. There are no other choices."

Thus, one sees how fairy tales, myths and fables, all different genres and aspects of folklore have been political carriers of social and cultural codes. These traditionally handed down narratives are not simply stories but they represent the genderized views of the patriarchal society where women are made aware of their given place, role, identity and fixed position as prescribed by man. This is the basis of gender construction in society in which one sex is privileged and another marginalized causing disparity. Feminist are wary about this artificial sexual division between man and woman, and assert that women can live a life of their own free of male interference and domination over their self, identity. Feminist re-writing of these stories is to revamp and relocate the voice of women in such cultural representations which was earlier made from the point of view of man in which women were not only relegated to the marginal position but also reminded of their subordinate role as man's other. Canadian feminist writers while rewriting such stories challenge the image of women as submissive to men, and make a call to women to rise out of their slumber and shake off the bondage of heterosexual marriage where women are enslaved. Some of them therefore openly advocate lesbianism in their recreated narratives for more freedom of women to end the physical, mental, emotional and sexual oppression of woman by man. Thus, they have broken the conventional notions of women passed on from one generation to another so as to create new models for women to emulate. To conclude with the words of Kaarina Kailo: "By rewriting the very stories that controlled us in so many ways, we can finally have our cake and eat it too. We can kiss ourselves awake from the hundreds of years of fruitful waiting, the miracles that don't happen, the rescuers that more often than not leave women in the lurch. Stories have the power to reawaken our senses, in all the senses of the word. Stories are . . . our gynocentric wonderlands. They promise hope and healing if we take the time to reconsider the values we transmit through them to children, if we take the time to UN-think." (92)

Works Cited

Andermahr, Sonya. "The Politics of Separatism and Lesbian Utopian Fiction," *New Lesbian Criticism: Literary and Cultural Readings*, ed. Sally Munt. New York: Columbia University Press, 1992.

Bettelheim, Bruno. *The Uses of Enchantment: The Meaning and Importance of Fairy Tales*. New York: Alfred A. Knopf, 1976.

Branicky, Melissa. "Rapunzel, Rapunzel, Let Down Your Hair . . .," *Room of One's Own: A Space for Women's Writing*, 17:1 (March 1994).

Dégh, Linda. Folk Narrative. Richard M. Dorson, ed. *Folklore and Folklife: An Introduction*. Chicago: The U of C. Press, 1972.

Greene, Elizabeth "Cinderella's Daughters," *Room of One's Own: A Space for Women's Writing*, 17:1 (March 1994).

Grimm, the Brothers and Hans Christian Anderson. The Little Mermaid. *The Best Fairy Tales*. London: Octopus Books, 1984.

Hines, Virginia Lee. "An Old Story," *Room of One's Own: A Space for Women's Writing* 17:1 (March 1994) 33-34.

Kailo, Kaarina. "Refusing to Hold Our Tongues: Women's Folklore, Women's Orality as Self-Recovery," *Room of One's Own: A Space for Women's Writing*, 17:1 (March 1994).

Kudchedkar, Shirin. "Feminist Voices from Indian and Canada," *Feminist Spaces: Cultural Readings from India and Canada,* ed. Malashri Lal. New Delhi: Allied, 1997.

Rankin, Pauline. "A Mermaid Tail," *Room of One's Own: A Space for Women's Writing* 17:1 (March 1994) .

Rooney, Frances. "Tree and Bear," *Room of One's Own: A Space for Women's Writing*, 17:1 (March 1994).

Sankey, Gretchen. "Re-viewing the Life and Times of Little Red Riding Hood," *Room of One's Own: A Space for Women's Writing*, 17:1 (March 1994).

Schwenk, Lorna. "Plucking," *Room of One's Own: A Space for Women's Writing*, 17:1 (March 1994).

Steinborn, Tamara. "Eve Revisited," *Room of One's Own: A Space for Women's Writing*, 17:1 (March 1994) 35.

Biblical Patterns in Lepcha Folk Literature

TSHERING NAMGYAL BHUTIA
Sikkim Government College

Takeover of a heathen culture is always easier by appropriating their auspicious days and their legends and myths. It spares them a cultural shock and makes the new religion seem more acceptable. Conversion also works on a similar footing. To soften the blow, the existing literature is appropriated and reworked to show signs of a similarity, in some of their mythical stories, with the stories in the Bible. This is just one of the weapons in their arsenal, albeit an effective one. The other is to portray the local heathen deities in an unfavorable light and their customs as inhuman and evil, thereby showcasing Christianity as redemption. A form of order amidst disorder. This pattern is visible in most tribal conversions throughout the erstwhile British colonies, be it in Asia, Africa or America. This paper attempts to trace the influence of the early missionaries which led to a large-scale conversion of the aboriginal Lepcha community of Sikkim into Christianity and also the possible impact it could have had in a reworking of their local literature along biblical lines.

The Lepchas are an aboriginal tribe of Sikkim thought to have migrated and settled here from the lower regions of Tibet. Some also speculate that they migrated from the Khasia hills. Despite the ambiguities in the account of their migration, it can be firmly accepted that they were among the first tribes to settle in Sikkim. Originally, practitioners of the Mon faith, the Lepcha at present have mostly converted to institutional religions like

Buddhism and Christianity. The first wave of conversion can be traced back to the impact of large-scale migration of the Tibetan Red hat sect who are called the Bhutias today. As a subsequent result of the conflict between the Yellow hat and the Red hat sects for supremacy in Tibet and the eventual migration of the latter into Sikkim, the more docile Lepchas were brought face to face with a more dominant and aggressive tribe. The Bhutias captured land and property and installed a King and also converted parts of the Lepcha population to Buddhism. The second wave came centuries later and was more subtle in its approach. Relying mostly on their missionaries, the Christian church sought conversion of local populations in far-flung regions of the world. Their modus operandi was similar in Sikkim. The missionary inroad was first made into Darjeeling, which was already a British outpost by the deed of grant signed by the Chogyal of Sikkim on 1 February 1835. The Start mission (1841), named after Reverend William Start, translated and published the gospel in the Lepcha and Nepali languages. An article written by Anira Phipon Lepcha in *The Church History Review* states, "probably the oldest Lepcha printed book, to have survived to the present day, is *The Book of Genesis* and parts of *Exodus* in Lepcha, Baptist Mission church, 1849, translated by Niebel." They can be credited with rescuing the Lepcha language from near extinction.

The Lepcha origin story finds a striking parallel with the *Book of Genesis* in *The Old Testament.* Itbu-Moo, the great mother creator of the Lepchas can be equated with God, the creator of the world in the Bible. Just as God created the world and eventually created Adam, so did Itbu-Moo create the river, the forests, the mountains and everything else on earth and then created Tukbothing, to lord over it all. In the Bible, God creates Eve, out of Adam's rib, to be a companion to him; similarly Nazong Nyu was created out of Tukbothing's marrow to be his companion and helpmate. There are slight variations as to the first man and woman in Lepcha accounts of the origin story. Authors like Pema Wangchuk and Mita Zulca in their book *The Sacred Summit* accept Tukbothing and Nazong Nyu as the first man and woman respectively. This view is also supported by Albert Foning in his novel, *Lepchas, My Vanishing Tribe*. By popular belief, among the Lepchas, Foodongthing and Nazongnyo are considered to be the first man and woman. Despite the variations, what cannot be contested is the similarity that the Lepcha origin story bears with the biblical account of genesis. It logically follows that Mayel Lyang (the birthplace of the Lepchas) is just an aboriginal version of Paradise.

The biblical story of the Tower of Babel likewise bears a close similarity with Tallom Partam, the story of the erection of the earthen tower in Daramdin by the Lepchas. In Babel, after the great flood, a united humanity, speaking a common language, decided to build a city and a tower that would reach up to the heavens in order to secure themselves in the event of another great flood; similarly the Lepchas decided on constructing an earthen staircase in Daramdin which would lead them to the heaven above. Their reason to do so is, probably, entirely different. The Lepchas' attempt consisted in stacking an earthen pot on top of another. The similarities between the two stories do not end here; rather it gets more interesting. In Babel, God witnessed this united effort of human beings and was threatened by the realization that they could achieve anything as long as they stood together. With the intention to disunite them, God confounded their language and the people could no longer understand one another. He also scattered them to different parts of the earth, thus achieving his purpose. Although a direct role of God cannot be traced in the Lepcha folk story but here too a confusion in language becomes the root cause of their failure. Upon nearing the end of their endeavour, a confusion arose when the message relayed by the person on top was incorrectly received by the person at the bottom and he smashed the lower pots, bringing the staircase crashing down to earth. Although not explicitly stated but a divine hand can be inferred as causing the confusion.

Flood myths and legends are normally born out of local flood stories which are then raised to the level of myths of dissolution. No historical account is available for the story of the flood in Lepcha folklore leading one to surmise a biblical intrusion with parallels to the story of the great flood in the Bible. Although in Genesis seven it is God who commands Noah to take with him into the ark every species of birds and beasts to ensure their survival during the Great Flood that God intends to send to earth through forty days and forty nights of rain, in the Lepcha folk tale the flood is caused by the combined waters of Teesta and Rangit, two major rivers of Sikkim, which flowed backwards and flooded the valleys. The Lepchas climbed higher up to escape the flood but the waters kept rising. It is then that Tendong hill, much like a Noah figure, bent down and carried the Lepcha people and rose higher and higher, thus saving them from the flood. To this day Tendong hill is revered and an annual festival is held to celebrate this event.

Although, slight variations can be perceived in these stories when compared to their counterparts in the Bible, but it is probably to give these stories a local colouring and make them more digestible. There is also a counter view that these myths and legends existed independently before the advent of Christianity and is also considered one of the reasons why the Lepcha tribe was attracted towards Christianity. This view supposes the parallels and similarities between the folklores and the stories of the *Old Testament* to have been an important reason for the Lepchas to readily identify with the new religion and eventually adopt it. But it should be mentioned here that one of the age-old methods of the missionaries to secure conversion has been to appropriate the local myths and legends. This is clearly traceable in the Epistles of Paul where Saint Paul quotes pagan poetry three times to convince the wise men of the Greek Areopagus in Athens about the prophecy inherent in their poetry pointing to the advent of Christianity. However difficult it may be to confirm, with authority, the influence of the Bible in the shaping of these folklores, it is equally hard to deny the similarities and parallels that exist. The trajectory of the Lepcha tribe, relinquishing their ancestral faith and adopting Christianity is also a reality that lends credibility to such conjectures. It is upon researchers into this field that we must depend for a finality. Until then we can but weave patterns that fit our suppositions.

Works Cited

Doma, Yeshey. *Legends of the Lepchas*. Tranquebar, Westland, 2010.

Zulca, Mita and Wangchuk Pema. *Khangchendzonga: Sacred Summit.* Pema Wangchuk, Hill Side Press, Kathmandu, 2007.

Foning, A.R. *Lepcha, My Vanishing Tribe*. Sterling, 1987.

Church History Review. Church History Association of India. 2010

Bible stories from the Old Testament. www.learningscriptures.info

Frailty, thy Name is Woman!: Gender Politics in the Manipuri Folk Epic *Khamba-Thoibi*

PRAGYA MOIRANGTHEM
Ph.D. Research Scholar, Viswa Bharati

The world's great folk epics were produced during heroic days of the past centuries when the heroic exploits of great culture heroes were looked upon as models of valour and bravery. People emulated and identified themselves with such heroes who aroused in them strong communal and nationalistic feelings and ideals which could sustain the enduring interest and admiration of such epics that have existed in various forms, chanted, narrated, sung, recited and/or performed. American folklorist R.M. Dorson rightly says: "Epic poems grew out of appropriate cultural conditions, the so-called Heroic Age bridging nomadic and sedentary stages of civilization, a pre-literate era when birds celebrated the deeds of great warriors" (1-2). From the heroic deeds and social functions and image of the society seen in such epics it will not be wrong to say that oral epics cherished universality of patriarchal social order and structure based on hierarchy, gender differentiation, discrimination and domination of women by men along the sexual binarism. No wonder women's exclusivity from participation is determined by the definition of woman as a weaker sex and her body is her destiny. Sexual binarism further leads to her subordination exacerbated by feminine attributes. In epics, great wars, heroic fights where kings, warriors, and their mighty enemies are involved count for more and where the world of women is less visible in public counts for less. The *Iliad,* the *Odyssey*, the *Mahabharata*, the *Ramayana*, the *Nibelungenlied*, *Beowulf*, the *Kalevela* are a few of the widely known epics of the world where heroic actions are performed by the heroes. Besides being sung or narrated by bards as verbal or expressive literary genre, the epic domain lies more or less in man's world as the subject indicates. In her book, *Studying Women's Writing*, Ruth Sherry makes an apt remark: "Some subjects (waging war, life at sea, struggles for political power) seem to exclude or minimize women characters because for the most part women have not, historically, been central or public participants in these activities" (2). Epic is a space where women's lives, ideas, emotions and preoccupations are given less importance and the dominant role is that of men rather than that of women. It is in its entirety a display of patriarchal authority and male solidarity and subordination of women as "Other" pitted against the absolutism of male, as Simone de Beauvoir says that in a patriarchal and androcentric world the social construct of the polarity of the male and female spheres is normal. She is relational and he is autonomous. Literature, oral or written as cultural product, bears testimony to this social phenomenon.

In our context, by gender politics we mean the power-structured relations between man and woman. Gender involves the socially and culturally constructed attributes which are not necessarily connected with a person's maleness or femaleness. However, gender studies emphasizes the two distinct categories of female and feminine as sites of gender oppression as they are often subsumed by patriarchy in order that the perpetuation of woman's suppression continues for the benefit of man by defining female in terms of femininity. It envisages the end of the mythology of gender as a divide between the sexes through transformation of the various oppressive and deep-seated norms and social organizations of patriarchy, For in history, culture and scripture a woman is treated as a frail, impure and inferior being, inferior to man. One is to see how in history women have been given a sub-human status: "'The female is a female by virtue of certain lack of qualities,' said Aristotle; 'we should regard the female nature as afflicted with a natural defectiveness.' And St. Thomas for his part pronounced woman to be an 'imperfect man,' an 'incidental' being. This is symbolized in Genesis where Eve is depicted as male from what Bossuet called 'a supernumerary bone' of Adam" (de Beauvoir 15-16).

Added to these are female nature and essentialism as inseparable from her sex/gender. Gender provides "pre-defined and pre-ordained spheres of activity, modes of dress, forms of deference, expectations about behaviour, and even parameters of design" and "gender assignments are culturally and socially powerful and produce fundamental differences in the world view for women and men, girls and boys" (Bottigheimer 2). For a woman these are shackles and fetters in her progression through the various stages of life. Gender criticism is a part of gender studies which developed in the 1980s. Gender studies more often than not "overlap with *feminist criticism*, *gay studies* and *lesbian studies*" and perhaps what distinguishes gender studies is "their special attention to the roles of males, and of varying conceptions of masculinity in the course of social, political, and artistic history" (Abrams and Harpham 119). Gender questions are extremely pertinent to the folk narrative research/ study. The answer as to why they are so is provided by Bottigheimer in her introduction to *Folklore and Gender*: "In the process of folk narrative production, every story component and every analytic process is fundamentally conditioned by gender. Voicing within tales depends to a very great extent on the gender of the voice that tells a tale. Does the heroine speak? What does she say? Is there a heroine at all? Is there a hero? What does he do? Each of these narrative acts depends on social patterning within a society." (5)

To discuss gender politics is to talk about power in relation to both men and women—the roles and practices they engage in the public as well as private spheres. In the present paper an investigation into the subtle and intricate workings of gender politics in the *Khmaba-Thoibi* Manipuri (Meitei) oral epic is attempted. The *Khamba-Thoibi* is the only secular heroic epic echoing a long tradition of Meitei culture centring round the social and cultural activities, customs and traditions of Moirang on the fringe of the Loktak lake, a glittering gem of silvery water dotted in the centre of the valley of Manipur. It will be a sound argument that the epic was a product of the pre-literate society of Moirang. It will be of some interest to enter into the dialogue about the possible origin of this heroic epic. Suniti Kumar Chatterji maintains that the epic "began to be treated in Old Meitei ballads from the middle of the twelfth century. The lovers [Khamba and Thoibi] lived about 1100, during the rule of king Loyamba [sic] (153) However, King Loyumba reigned in Kangleipak in 1074-1122 according to *Cheitharol Kumbaba* (Royal Chronicle). If they lived during the time of King Loyumba and their story was sung from the middle of the twelfth century what Suniti Chatterji says is convincing. But to look at the epic from the point of view of historical evidence—all the events chronicled in the epic, both actual and fictional or some future interpolations—seemed to have occurred during the time of Moirang King Chingkhu Telheiba, and Thoibi being the daughter of the King's younger brother, Chingkhuba, a powerful courtier. And the King and his famous courtiers are mentioned all the time. Further investigation shows that King Chingkhu Telheiba of Moirang was a contemporary of Kanglei King Meidingu Tangbi Lanthaba whose rule dates from 1302 to 1324. Evidently, the historical linkage of the story of Khamba and Thoibi is irrefutable. Generally epic stories sprang up after the real historical events took place one hundred to two hundred years ago. But that depends on the nature of the society and the presence of highly innovative and talented minstrels. In certain cases, the possibility of early start of such narratives is fictionally seen in the *Odyssey* as on his way back Odysseus hears the blind bard, Demodocus, sing his heroic deeds in Troy. In Meitei society a heroic ballad in praise of Major Paona Brajabashi, the fallen hero of the Khongjom War immediately after Manipur was defeated by the British in 1891 started to be sung by a singer named Dhobi Leinou. Soon his style was known as Khongjon Parba, and bards applied this singing style to the *Khamba-Thoibi* epic with the accompaniment of a musical instrument called *Dholok*. Originally epic is sung in Manipur on an ancient musical instrument *Pena*. Historical dating of the origin of the folk epic needs more discussion but the matter is not pursued further in this paper.

Both Khamba and Thoibi are victims of class and gender discriminations. Khamba, an obscure young man, is a descent of Khuman dynasty. On his birth both parents were dead leaving him with his infant sister, Khamnu. Orphaned as they were, seldom do the people in Moirang remember their parentage in course of time and started living in abject poverty taking shelter at whichever place that welcomed them. But Khamba by virtue of his extraordinary look, talent, strength, simplicity, honesty, valour and firm stand earns the love and sympathy of all, and rises to fame in the whole kingdom now able to draw the unfailing attention of the princess, Thoibi, who also possesses all feminine virtues but she is an embodiment of strong feminine protest against injustice, repressive measures and seen as opposed to any kind of forcible imposition of rules and norms against her will and determination. At times she plays prank on Khamba too to the extent that the latter is on the verge of being punished but she won't allow to let it go further by her tact, ready wit and mesmerizing persuasive discourse.

Being a princess Thoibi lives in a male-dominated courtly world where strict rules of conduct and decorum are created by the male heads ascertaining social (as well as gender) hierarchy and the gender roles that both men and women have to entail.

But Thoibi is certainly not the damsel in distress waiting for her knight in shining armour nor is she the mute spectator of the go-ings on. Throughout the epic she is the unbeatable free spirit; she takes charge of her own life asserting her position as a woman and bringing herself to the centre from the marginalized position to which women are subjected in a heavily gendered, normative patriarchal society. In the absolute male-dominating patriarchal world of Moirang Thoibi's voice is the only female voice that prevails upon the public (or what one may call the 'masculine') sphere. In the episode of *Kang Shannaba*, Thoibi prays to God Thangjing asking Him to deliver the dice (*Kang*) to Khamba (unnoticed by everyone) in a bid to test whether or not she would marry Khamba. The dice is kept concealed in Khamba's dress (as engineered by God Thangjing) but on her complaint that the same is lost the courtiers frisk men folk one after another. When Khamba's turn comes he protests his innocence, meanwhile Thoibi senses something ugly may take place and cautions the noblemen:

> Alas, for God's sake, nobleman, why, pray—
> The game I initiate today for the girls,
> Why go out of hand for the land's sake!
> Restrain yourself hurt not Moirang brethren
> Assail not for the Kang I better lose
> For my lost thing why subject one to frisking
> Don't do any where others can point
> To my name, so saying she calms all down.
>
> (*Kang Shannaba* 38)

After Khamba's outstanding performance in the *Kangjei* match, Chaoba Nongthonba demands his parentage and whereabouts to which he gives no proper reply out of shame. Enraged by the improper reply Nongthonba orders that Khamba reveal his true identity immediately lest he be thrashed. Thoibi sees that it is a gross abuse of power and sends her maid Senu to Chaoba pleading for Khamba. At this Chaoba dismisses Senu: "Senu go and tell your princess, hear me!/ You women know nothing about State affairs!/For a kingdom we have strict rules" (Kangjei 65). Thoibi is reminded that as a woman she has no say on matters of public domain. Speaking is power laden public affair and not in the least women's private sphere. Simone de Beauvoir in *The Second Sex* had famously said "One is not born, but rather becomes, a woman" (295). Patriarchy tries to keep woman in her place, persistently reminding her that because of her sex she has to remain faithful and bear the social, political inscriptions silently. Although male singers praise and endow Thoibi with feminine virtues, they also refrain from making comments at such moments. In order to fit in to the society Thoibi has to 'become' a woman for that is the expected gender role assigned to her as a female. She has to broil in the circumscribed space meant for her sex.

Likewise, on many occasions, Thoibi wishes to see Khamba when he displays his flair in public events, competitions where the deceitful villain Nongban is his rival who by virtue of his father being a nobleman in the king's court and himself a nobleman too, and a strong contender for Thoibi, is all out to do harm to Khamba. But women are excluded from such events, their appearance in such events is prohibited. On many occasions Thoibi expresses how she is disadvantaged because of her sex: "It's woeful, frailty, thy name is woman!" (*Lamjel* 250). The arrow-shooting ritual festival is exclusively for men, no woman is permitted to witness it. For this festival Thoibi presents Khamba's apparel, made by her, but social prohibition condemns her to her place. She protests: "Being born a female/ I am not to see, oh how he appears/ I long to see" (*Ukai Kappa* 461). Again the same motif appears in another canto. Women can't go hunting but when the ritual of hunting in which the kill is to be offered to God Thangjing Thoibi again laments: "My dear Senu! To be a woman is sorrowful/I'm dying to go hunting, why only man/I wish I had been a man" (*Torbung Shatanba* 532). These are some instances when Thoibi resents her fate of a woman and also takes strong exception to patriarchal authority imposed on women's liberty. Patriarchy that creates sexual difference is an elaborate system of domination of one sex over another. Restrictions imposed on her movement and curtailment of rights on the basis of sexual difference become very explicit in the epic all of which strongly reject woman's public space, for she is given her due in the society. She is not represented, her voice is not heard, all laws are made by men, women have to follow them, she is underprivileged. A woman under patriarchy is a slave no less. Women could not protect the society, women could not earn income, women could not be in court to decide cases, women could not decide a woman's case. A woman in patriarchal society is a dependent, her position is no better than that of a slave. Who takes cares of: child bearing?—a woman; child rearing?—a woman; weaving?—a woman; cleaning, washing?—a woman; domestic chores? a woman—an angel in the family. In spite of this, does she get her due? She is still treated as the Other of man. She is called when some order is to be given. Patriarchy is such an organized social structure made over the years and to challenge its authority became unthinkable generations ago. Man was the master who "exercised tyrannical authority, which exalted his pride—and he turned against woman. Everything he gained he gained against her; the more powerful he became, the more she declined" (de Beauvoir 110).

However, bards have not painted Thoibi as a submissive woman character all through. She has a vital role in the epic for she has to save Khamba and fight for justice and both would not be so simple because that entails a stiff fight against male authority. In the canto *Shamu Khongyet* at dead of night Khamba is tightly bound to the foot of an elephant and dragged in the market square place orchestrated by Thoibi's father Yubaraj Chingkhuba, and Nongban so as to remove the earthly obstacle to Nongban's wishful thinking about marrying Thoibi. When Goddess Panthoibi informs Thoibi in her dream about the murder attempt on Khamba by her father, she comes rushing quick as a flash to Khamba's rescue. Enraged at the murderous attack on her lover she draws her two knives and hurls them at Nongban, her father having fled from the scene on seeing Thoibi in the distance crying for revenge. But due to divine intervention Nongban is not hit with the knives directly. The exposure leads to the trial of Chingkhuba and Nongban. Further complications develop when the elephant trainer is tried and convicted for his unauthorized use of the elephant. At this Thoibi is intent on saving the life of the wrongly implicated man and thus pleads for the man in a message to the King and his noblemen

> "Mighty King, Thonglen Mantri, Nongthomba
> The deposition in the court today
> By Takhen Sharunghanba was true, I know
> Yet despite it you pass death sentence
> Let Khamnu and Thoibi be killed in his place
> Or withhold the verdict O Mighty king
> I entreat you in supplication
> In case he dies, Khamnu, Thoibi will take
> Life where he dies," so says the letter.
>
> (*Shamukhongi Bichar* 75-6)

On the spur of the moment Thoibi awakens the King and his courtiers, and soon the accused is freed. A woman though she is, her pleadings prevail upon the king and his royal court. That does not, however, give a blueprint for gender equality nor is it a strong message of female empowerment. But at the most her voice is heard. But unlike her, all other women characters in the epic, are seldom seen. What more distinctions she has are that: she is not a silent receiver of the impositions of patriarchy; all her life she stands against injustice; and, she challenges the marriage institution and polygamy.

She goes by the individual worth of a person and not of false values and outward show. Her father Chingkhuba repeatedly insists that she marry Nongban, she stands firm by her integrity and refuses to marry a person who is not her choice. She is an exception to what Simone de Beauvoir observes: "But in the patriarchal regime she is the property of her father, who marries her off to suit himself" (115). This is exactly what Chingkhuba tries to do but by no means Thoibi allows commodification of woman. She remains unbending when pressure in the form of punishment is given to her to the maximum extent of her banishment to Kabo (the then Burma) where she suffers servitude at the Tumu Lakpa's. In order to save her identity, her individual choice, selfhood and self-respect and above all to prove her ability to suffer for true love she chooses exile rather than submitting to her father's will and becoming the wife of Nongban. For her knowledge, wisdom and practical experience she deserves to be the King of Moirang who has no heir to succeed him yet due to her gender she is denied the right to the throne. She does not shout slogans for the gender equality nor does she bear banners against sexual oppression; she does exude power as a human woman in a world surrounded by fierce norms of patriarchy. She makes sure that she finds herself a place in the Moirang society and that she has a voice of her own that finds its way to the public sphere from time to time. She suffers, resists such patriarchal norms, social and domestic impositions until she is united with Khamba, a hero of her choice.

It is evident from the above discussion that Thoibi being the sole princess of Moirang does enjoy certain autonomy. However, it is important to examine the other female characters in the epic because talking about gender "is a constant reminder of the other categories of difference, such as race and class, that structure our lives and texts, just as theorizing gender emphasizes the parallels between feminist criticism and other forms of minority discourse" (Showalter 3). Unlike Thoibi Senu, Khamnu, the fifteen wives of the King and the nine wives of Yubaraj Chingkhuba do not have a voice, they remain quite invisible most of the time. Khamnu, Khamba's elder sister, is perhaps the wisest and most far-sighted woman character in the epic but she is not given any proper voice in the public sphere. When the furious Yubaraj Chingkhuba passes the order that his only daughter be sent into exile, none of the nine wives has a say on the grievous matter. None of them has the power or the courage to protest having been rendered powerless by a single patriarch. They give in to the wishes of Chingkhuba even though not one of them supports the decision. While Yengkhurangbi, the blood mother of Thoibi, eats with her daughter the last meal before exile, Chingkhuba shouts that the hand that shares food with Thoibi shall be chopped off. Shocked and mortified Yengkhurangbi insists on her having the last meal with Thoibi at which Chingkhuba threatens that she would be sent back to her parents. Feminist critics are wary about such patriarchal oppressive practices that reduce women to the biological female only. Toril Moi remarks: "patriarchal oppression consists of imposing certain social standards of femininity on all biological women, in order precisely to make us believe that the chosen standards for femininity are *natural*." Thoibi's mothers have become puppets of patriarchy, they have been tamed and domesticated by the institutionalized patriarchal norms.

One significant observation may also be made at this point. Like women, man in patriarchal society is also not excluded from acting to fulfil the social expectations. Look at the character of Nongban who is often and unanimously hailed as the villain of the epic by critics and scholars alike. One should not overlook the fact that he too is a victim of the very same patriarchal system of the society. We are aware that certain social standards are also set for men, the non-adherence of which would "diminish or threaten their own manliness" (Showalter 7). Before Khamba became the talk of the town, Nongban was well received by the people for his strength, fighting skills, and prowess. He was the alpha male in Moirang but with Khamba occupying the centre stage, Nongban's position is on the wane until his final fall. Central to the plot complications, conflicts and rivalry between Nongban and Khamba there is Thoibi for whose favour the two have become mortal enemies. Nongban is infatuated with Thoibi and conversely Thoibi loves Khamba. Khamba reciprocates Thoibi's love for him and that complicates matters. Chingkhuba takes advantage of the situation and manipulates Nongban into proving his 'masculinity':

> Say Nongban, are you sure?—Lord, I am firm
> Nongban, let us kill Khamba for without that
> Marrying my daughter! It's impossible.
>
> (Shamu-Khong 544)

Nongban goes overboard in proving his worth as the ultimate alpha male in Moirang. It is only when he is fatally wounded by the tiger (with no chance of survival) that he finally speaks out:

> Dear friend Khamba! All that I did you wrong
> I recalled them all, friend. I knew all.
> It's not that I saw nothing, forgive me.
> We are the players on the theatre
> All this is the action done by us both
> But alas it was not a pleasant affair.
> It was indeed a game of rivalry, dear friend.
>
> (Akonba Pannung Changba 1016)

This is one of the most poignant moments in the epic. Nongban finally proves that he is not the only villain who has used all foul and evil means that have caused untold suffering to Khamba. Trying to fit himself into the male specific pre-existent social image of man he pushes himself to his own doom.

To conclude, the above discussion has shown that the analysis of gender politics in the *Khamba-Thoibi* folk epic can bring forth new insights into perspectives in its criticism. However, a more thorough analysis is still needed in order to highlight the intricacies of how exactly gender functions in the text. In the epic Thoibi is seen everywhere, all actins revolve round her and adulations are poured upon her yet she suffers the innate femininity patriarchy inscribes on her and her sex. She sizes up any situation at times with more strength uncommon to a woman than that of man but she finds obstacles and fetters by her being a woman. She is a symbol of a subjugated and not an emancipated woman. Her society is not yet ready to give women their due on an equal basis without sexual prejudice. Such an epic of enormous size having about 34,000 lines with 43 books in its written form, and in the oral performatory for one month by skilled singers much still remains to be discussed on this subject.

Works Cited

Abrams, M.H. and Geoffrey Galt Harpham. *A Handbook of Literary Terms*. New Delhi: Cengage Learning, 2009.

Beauvoir, Simone de. *The Second Sex*. London: Vintage, 1997.

Bottigheimer, B. Ruth. "Introduction: Gender and Folk Narrative," Lalita Handoo and Ruth B. Bottighmeimer, ed. *Folklore and Gender*. Mysore: Zooni Publications, 1999.

Dorson, Richard M. "Introduction," Felix J. Oinas ed., *Heroic Epic and Saga: An Introduction to the World's Great Folk Epics*. Bloomington: Indiana U. P., 1978.

Moi, Toril. *Sexual/ Textual Politics*. London: Routledge, 1995.

Sherry, Ruth. *Studying Women's Writing: An Introduction*. London: Edward Arnold, 1988.

Showalter, Alaine ed. *Speaking of Gender*. New York: Routledge, 1989.

Singh, Hijam Anganghal. *Khamba-Thoibi Sheireng*. Imphal: Akoijam Offset Printing Works, 2013. All quotations are from this work in Manipuri, my translation.

Sandrembi Chaisra, a Manipuri Cinderella: Global Character and Local Variants

S. SANATOMBI
Department of Manipuri, Manipur University, Imphal

Before we start to properly study the proposed topic we ought to know what type of story is known as a Cinderella tale. Scholars in the West have cited Marian Roalfe Cox's *Cinderella* (1893) as the "first extensive investigation ever made of a folktale" (Thompson 127) in which she made a study of as many as 345 variants of the Cinderella tale. When Thompson in his book, *The Folktale* (1946), discussed Marian Roalfe Cox's *Cinderella* he categorically defined this tale type known as Cinderella: "In Cinderella the heroine is abused by her stepmother and step-sisters. Her name is always connected in some way with ashes (Cindrillon, Aschenputtel, or the like), indicating her lowly position in the household. The poor girl receives supernatural aid, sometimes from her dead mother, or from a tree on the mother's grave, or from an animal (often a reincarnation of the mother), or from a fairy godmother. In some versions the helpful animal is killed, and a tree springs up which magically provides beautiful clothes for the girl." (*ibid.*)

Research in Cinderella cycle brings out the existence of this tale type extensively in Europe, Asia, Africa. The next work on Cinderella is Anna Birgitta Rooth's *The Cinderella Cycle* (1951), a study of seven hundred Cinderella tales collected by her, displaying the variants of the Cinderella tale. Commenting on Cox's work, she writes: Cox's "intention was only to give a collection of Cinderella tales grouped in some natural types. As a starting point for further studies in the subject, her work about Cinderella is most important to students of folktales" (14). But the Cinderella tale is as repetitive as it is diverse, that within this unique structure there are subtypes and multiple variants. Marked by a variety of elements Cinderella tales may be of One Move or Two Moves where the story develops still further with additions and extended elements. Within the same frame it has a dynamic character that is, the existence of different but wholly veritable subtypes. This is exemplified when Alan Dundes makes an appraisal of the works of both Miss Cox and Anna Birgitta Rooth: "Both Miss Cox and Professor Rooth were especially interested in distinguishing the separate but seemingly related forms of the story of Cinderella. This is demonstrated by the subtitle of the first work and the title of the second. The *Cinderella Cycle* refers to several distinct subtypes of the basic tale, that is, a veritable complex of different tales which apparently belong under one single rubric." (vii-viii)

A Cinderella tale type is so diversified that it may appear in one of the forms: AT 510A. *Cinderella*; AT 510 *Cinderella and Cap o' Rushes*; AT 510A. *Cinderella* + AT 408 *The Three Oranges*; AT 510B. *The Dress of Gold, of Silver, and of Stars* (Cap o' Rushes); AT 511. *One-Eye, Two-Eyes, Three Eyes*; AT 511A. *The Little Red Ox*. However varied is the Cinderella tale it can be well fitted within the characteristic features of the Cinderella types as given above. Commenting on the number of different versions of Cinderella, Andrew Lang in his Introduction to Marian Roalfe Cox's *Cinderella* says: "As far as I can see, the number of possible combinations resulting in a story recognizably similar to Cinderella are infinite" (viii). Before we come to the study of a Manipuri Cinderella we still require to know the evolution of the proper study of the Cinderella tale. Miss Cox's analysis was focused on the classification of the Cinderella tales. That proved indeed a pathfinder in future folklore research. Both Cox and Rooth's works are, however, devoted to "distinguishing the separate but seemingly related forms of the story of Cinderella" (*ibid.*). While analyzing the subtypes and variants in the European Cinderella types Rooth covers among others the Indo-Chinese, Chinese and Indian variants which became a landmark in furthering research in Cinderella cycle. Another great work in addition to the American and European pioneering research work on Cinderella was the publication of Nai Tung Ting's *The Cinderella Cycle in China and Indo-China* in 1974 by FF Communications. Again the book, *Cinderella: A Casebook* (1982), edited by Alan Dundes, extends the horizon of one hundred years of research in Cinderella with new perspectives. According to this book European collection of different versions of Cinderella types started as early as Basile's *Pentamerone* (1634-36), Perrault's *Cindrillon* (1697) and Grimm's *Aschenputtel* (1812). Based on such collections and his own research Stith Thompson remarks, "This story of Cinderella appears in not fewer than five hundred versions in Europe alone" (127). The question as to how this tale type spread over vast areas of the world has still confounded folklorists. A fascinating discovery in Cinderella research is that all types available in different world cultures have striking similarities whether they are European or Asia origins. While talking of the similarities their differences are also equally interesting.

Scholars are of the view that "Chinese literary version of Cinderella has been reported from the ninth century after Christ" (*ibid.* 126). Turning to the Indian Cinderella: it is noted that not much extended study has been carried out so far. In her classification of the Cinderella tale Rooth includes a Kashmiri variant under Type AB. E. Sidney Hartland's "Notes on Cinderella" in *Cinderella: A Casebook* takes up the "masculine as well as feminine Cinderella" (67) in the folktales of Santhals. The earliest of the Indian folklorists who distinguished himself in the study of Cinderella is Professor Praphulladatta Goswami of Gauhati University from the North East India. He wrote an article, entitled

"The Cinderella Motif in Assamese Folktales" in 1947, earlier than the work of Anna Bergitta Rooth (1951). He further discussed the Assamese Cinderella in his book, *Ballads and Tales of Assam* (1960), where he recounts the views and findings of Rooth and Anderson. It will be significant to note the correspondence of Professor Goswami with Professor Walter Anderson of Kiel University, Germany, when the former did his research in Assamese Cinderella, "Teja and Teji." Professor Anderson made this useful observation that "Teja and Teji" is a combination of Cinderella + Three Oranges as Professor Goswami writes: "When Professor Anderson found the text of 'Teja and Teji' he wrote to me: 'This text is exceedingly precious for me, for it shows that Assam has been the bridge by which the combination Cinderella + Three Oranges has wandered from India to Indo-China (Assam, the Cham people Cambodia), and later on to China and Korea. Especially the words 'O bird if indeed you're my queen, alight on my shoulder (or: slide into my sleeve),' related in most of the Indo-Chinese and Chinese versions, but absolutely unknown westward of Assam, appear for the first time in your Assamese text.'" (160)

While in the course of his research Professor Goswami made a reference to the Burmese tale "The Big Tortoise" (in the book by Maung Htin Aung. *Folktales of Burma*, 1980) which contains very similar elements as in "Teja and Teji." He introduced the tale to Prof Anderson who then made this comment: "The tale 'The Big Tortoise' is really a precious version of the combination Cinderella + Three Oranges" (*ibid.*). Anderson's views on The Three Oranges (Type No. 408) were considered a great contribution to folklore scholarship. Stith Thompson owes a great deal to Professor Anderson for his contribution to the Cinderella scholarship. Thompson writes in his *The Types of the Folktale*: *The Three Oranges*. The quest for the orange princess. The false bride.

1. *The Old Woman's Curse*. A young prince insolently throws a stone and breaks an old woman's oil jar. She utters a curse: he is to fall in love with the three oranges (lemons, pomegranates, eggs).
2. *The Winning of the Orange Princess*. The prince sets out on the quest. An old woman (or other person) gives him good advice and after overcoming various obstacles he finds the three oranges. Out of the first orange comes a beautiful maiden, calls for water and dies. The same thing happens with the second orange. For the third orange, the prince has water ready and she remains alive. Since she is naked the prince leaves her hidden among the branches of a tree and goes to bring clothes for her.
3. *The Substitution of a Negress for the Orange Princess*. Under the tree there is a spring. A hideous negro slave (gypsy) comes to get water, thinks that the reflection of the heroine is her own and breaks her water jar since she is too beautiful to carry water. Orange Princess laughs and thus draws attention. The slave learns her story and turns her into a dove (fish etc.) and takes her place. The prince returns and though astonished at the sudden change marries the false bride.
4. *The Orange Princess as Dove*. The dove flies to a castle and asks the gardener (cook) about the prince and the false bride. The dove is captured and the prince is much pleased but the negress has the bird killed.
5. *The Orange Princess as Tree*. From the remains of the bird arises a tree. The prince is pleased but the false bride has it cut down.
6. *The Disenchantment of the Heroine*. A chip of the tree comes into the hands of an old woman. During her absence the orange princess assumes her earlier form and does the old woman's house work. Eventually she is surprised by the old woman.

7. *The Lovers' Reunion.* The prince finds the Orange Princess again; the false bride is hanged.

(Analysis furnished by Prof. Walter Anderson in Thompson 135-36)

II

The structures of Cinderella (AT 510A) and The Three Oranges (AT 408) were a result of dedicated research works of eminent folklorists of the world declared to have been highly authoritative guidelines for the study of the Cinderella tale types. In folklore studies variants are apparently an intrinsic characteristic of verbal art or oral narratives, and give an inexhaustible source of future investigation. Indeed these elements make the study of folklore highly refreshing for they lead to further ethnographic and contextual analysis. But the similarities within the same tale type will reveal the global nature of the tale living in different cultures. It is in this context that the paper tries to study a Manipuri Meitei folktale, *Sandrembi Chaisra* as a Cinderella type, a combination of "Cinderella + The Three Oranges." This tale does not come under any one of the categories such as *Cap o' Rushes*, AT 511 *One-Eye, Two Eyes, Three-Eyes*, although these are also still known as different versions of the Cinderella tale type. It will be proper to give the outline of the tale *Sandrembi Chaisra* before we proceed further:

> There were two widow co-wives. Both women had one daughter each. The senior co-wife's daughter was called Sandrembi, and the junior co-wife's Chaisra. Once the two co-wives were out fishing in the Silem lake, and as luck would have it Chaisra's mother caught only snakes and no fish, but Sandrembi's mother had a bagful of fishes caught. On their way back Chaisra's mother, full of jealousy, persuaded the senior co-wife to eat ripe figs, she climbed the tree asking Sandrembi's mother to lie down face up at the foot of the tree opening her mouth widely while keeping her eyes closed so that the ripe fig would come down into her mouth. But after the initial dropping of the fruit she poured snakes into the mouth of the senior co-wife leading to the instantaneous death of the latter. Chaisra's mother returned home after exchanging the

fishing bags, and she curtly said to Sandrembi in reply to her enquiry, "Your greedy mother went on fishing unconcerned about my request to go home." As the mother did not return home till late night Sandrembi fell asleep, and in her dream her dead mother appeared and told her that she was killed by the stepmother and that she had now become a tortoise which Sandrembi should come and take her home and keep her in a pot for seven days secretly so that she would return to her earlier human form. Sandrembi did everything as directed, but Chaisra stealthily saw it and demanded that the tortoise be cooked. The stepmother ordered Sandrembi to boil the tortoise, lest she would be severely dealt with. The tortoise was eaten by both stepmother and stepsister. Again in Sandrembi's dream her dead mother appeared and told her to collect the bones from the backyard and keep them wrapped up in a basket for seven days so that she could return to her earlier human form. But unable to resist temptation on the sixth day Sandrembi opened the basket and a dove instead of a human being appeared that flew away.

Years later Sandrembi and Chaisra grew up, and one day both went to fetch water, the former in her rough clothing and the latter dressed in her best clothes each carrying a container one an earthen and another a bronze respectively. While returning from the pond they encountered a king on horseback, who demanded water from Sandrembi's container. He had his fill of drink and away he went. Chaisra reported what had happened to her mother. The next day the two girls at the behest of Chaisra's mother exchanged their clothes and containers and went out to fetch water. The king came again, took away Sandrembi and soon rode fast. Sandrembi became a queen. Later on, after her first child birth, at the invitation of her stepmother and stepsister she came to take food together. Both women planned to kill Sandrembi and they did so by pouring hot water, and Sandrembi flew away transformed into a dove. Then Chaisra wearing Sandrembi's clothes and jewels in substitution of the queen, went to the palace where she stayed with the king, despite the king's questioning over the queen's strange appearance—how her eyes became sunk in the sockets, her eye-lashes grew longer and her heels cracked to which the false queen replied that her eyes went inside as she rubbed her eyes wiping the tears after she had cried long remembering her dead mother, hence the eyes went inside and the lashes appeared longer as a result and her heels cracked when she came running to feed her child. On the other hand, the dove transformed by Sandrembi sang to the king's gardener, "O King, Sandrembi is sitting on the branch of a tree but Chaisra sits glamorously on the throne." This was reported to the king by the gardener. The king came and called to the bird, "O bird, if you are my true queen, you alight and peck at the grains in my palm." The bird did as asked. Pleased, the king brought it home where he kept the bird hidden so that on the seventh day it would turn into Sandrembi. When the king went hunting Chaisra had the bird killed and cooked for the king. The enraged king did not eat the curry and threw it away in the backyard. From the bones of the bird a lemon tree grew in the backyard and bore a fruit. The gardener plucked it and brought it to eat, but kept forgetting. On the seventh day the lemon turned into Sandrembi. Unnoticed she kept the house clean and tidy, cooked food for the gardener in his absence. One day the gardener surprised the lemon queen. The king was apprised of the strange happening. He came and took her to the palace, where the claim and counter-claim of the two queens were heard. Unable to decide the case amicably the queens had a sword fight in which Sandrembi slew Chaisra. Thereafter a happy reunion of the king and queen took place.

An analysis of the motifs in this tale makes it clear that *Sandrembi Chaisra* is a combination of AT 510A + AT 408. The Three Oranges. First let us analyze how the tale approximates to the global elements of a Cinderella tale, AT 510A + AT 408. AT 510A Cinderella

1. *The Persecuted Heroine (a) The heroine is abused by her stepmother and stepsisters and (a^1) stays on the hearth and in the ashes and, (a^2) dresses in rough clothing* (Arnne-Thompson 1987: 175). Sandrembi is abused and subjected to hardships by her stepmother and stepsister. She does manual chores and is dressed in rough clothing.
2. *Magic Help. While she is acting as servant (at home) she is advised (a) by her dead mother* (*ibid.*). Sandrembi is

treated as a servant, forced to do things against her will at home by her stepmother and stepsister, and she is advised by her dead mother twice in her dream.

3. *Meeting the Prince* (*ibid.*). Sandrembi meets the king while fetching water (two times). In *Sandrembi Chaisra* the European (or Chinese etc.) Cinderella motifs like ball dance, and shoe test are not found. The meeting place has a pastoral setting. The hero marries the heroine through abduction (local variants).

Up to this point AT 510A Cinderella along with some local variants works. But after this, the post marriage development of the plot approximates it to AT 408 The Three Oranges nos. III to VII. Notice it again:

III. *The Substitution of a Negress for the Orange Princess. . . . The slave learns her story and turns her into a dove . . . and takes her place. The prince returns and though astonished at the sudden change marries the false bride* (136).

Sandrembi is invited to a feast by the stepmother and stepsister but is killed by pouring hot water and she turns into a dove. Chaisra wears Sandrembi's dress and jewellery, disguises herself as the queen and goes to the palace. The king becomes doubtful about the sudden change in the appearance of Sandrembi but is coaxed into believing that the false queen is Sandrembi.

IV. *The Orange Princess as Dove. The dove flies to a castle and asks the gardener (cook) about the prince and the false bride. The dove is captured and the prince is much pleased but the negress has the bird killed* (*ibid.*).

Sandrembi as dove flies to the palace, and tells the gardener that she is on the branch of a tree and Chaisra is on the throne. The king is informed of what had happened by the gardener; the king comes with a handful of rice in his hand, calls to the bird to alight on his hand and peck at the grains if she is the true queen. The dove obeys the king and pecks at the rice in his palm; the king catches the dove and brings it home. But the false queen kills it and cooks it for the king who without eating the curry throws it away in the backyard.

V. *The Orange Princess as Tree. From the remains of the bird arises a tree. The prince is pleased but the false bride has it cut down* (*ibid.*).

From the spot the curry is thrown a lemon (Heijang) tree grows and bears a fruit (In the Manipuri version the false queen does not cut it down).

VI. *The Disenchantment of the Heroine. A chip of the tree comes into the hands of an old woman. During her absence the orange princess assumes her earlier form and does the old woman's house work. Eventually she is surprised by the old woman* (*ibid.*).

The palace gardener while cleaning the backyard plucks the lemon fruit, keeps it in an earthen pot, and forgets to eat the fruit, and on the seventh day the fruit assumes the earlier form of Sandrembi, the queen. She does the old man's house work, cooks for him, and keeps the house clean and tidy. Eventually she is surprised by the old man, who informs the king.

VII. *The Lovers' Reunion. The prince finds the Orange princess again, the false bride is hanged* (*ibid.*)

The king brings Sandrembi to the palace and in order to decide on the claims of the two queens a test by a sword fight between them follows. In the fight Sandrembi kills Chaisra. The king and the queen are reunited and they would live happily ever after.

From the above analysis it is seen that *Sandrembi Chaisra* is a Cinderella type tale. It is well-fitted into the mould of international Cinderella tale type. If "Teja and Teji" and "The Big Tortoise" are praised as really precious versions of the combination Cinderella + Three Oranges then there is no reason as to why *Sandrembi Chaidra* should not be praised for the same characteristics. It will be of great significance if we see the closeness of these three versions through a display of the common motifs present in them:

Sandrembi Chaisra (Manipuri)	Teja and Teji (Assamese)	The Big Tortoise (Burmese)
Jr. co-wife kills Sr. co-wife.	Jr. co-wife kills Sr. co-wife	Husband kills first wife
The dead Sr. co-wife turns into tortoise	The dead Sr. co-wife turns into tortoise	The dead wife turns into tortoise
Spying on the step-sister	Spying on the step-sister	
Tortoise is cooked	Tortoise is cooked	Tortoise is cooked
The bones of the tortoise turn into a dove	On the grave of the tortoise gold and silver trees grow	On the grave of the tortoise gold and silver trees grow
Sandrembi is married to a king	A king marries the gold and silver trees' owner (Teji)	The king marries the gold and silver trees' owner
The queen is invited by the stepmother and stepsister to a feast but is killed by pouring hot water	Queen killed by step-sister by putting a thorn into head	The queen is invited by the stepmother and stepsister to a feast but is killed by pouring hot water
The queen is turned into a bird (dove)	The queen is turned into a bird (myna)	The queen is turned into a bird (white paddy bird)
Stepsister goes to the king in disguise	Stepsister goes to the king in disguise	Stepsister goes to the king in disguise
The bird sings a song about her grief and the false	The bird follows the false queen to the palace and is	

queen's happiness to the gardener. The king catches the bird and brings it home	caught by the king	
False queen kills the bird and cooks it for the king who throws away the curry in the back-yard		False queen kills the bird and cooks it for the king who buries the curry in the backyard
A lemon tree grows at the backyard		A quince fruit tree grows from the place where the curry was buried
The fruit turns into the former queen	The king removes the thorn from the head of the bird and it turns into the former queen	The fruit turns into the former queen
The true and the false queens are engaged in sword fight in which the false queen is slain	The king punishes the false queen	The true and the false queens are engaged in sword fight in which the false queen is slain
There is reunion of the king and the queen	There is reunion of the king and the queen	There is reunion of the king and the queen

In all these three tales we witness the repeated transformations of the heroine. This may be a unique pattern of the oriental Cinderella. It is because in the Chinese Cinderella also, we have seen the same repeated transformations of the heroine. Nai-Tung Ting writes: "After a dog has revealed the whereabouts of the heroine, and the latter has been happily married, her stepmother soaks her head in boiling water, thus causing her to lose first her golden hair and then her life. The sequel is the same as in the Modern Chinese Tradition. The heroine is transformed first into a bird, then into a rose bush, a tree, a bedstead, a splinter, a fritter, and finally herself again" (Ting 1974: 18).

From the above discussion it is seen that despite the presence of some motif variations the "functions" they perform have almost been identical. The plot develops almost the same in all these versions. These different versions that come out as a result of comparative analysis of such a tale type in different cultures, however, become highly provocative in folklore research.

The common traits that are prevalent in all Cinderella tales indicate that human beings irrespective of their race, nationality, and geographical factors are bound by certain common heritage, universally shared patterns and rhythms of life, birth, marriage, death, beliefs, customs, notions of good and evil, right and wrong, justice and injustice, love and hate, all an expression of "the mental health of humankind" (Lule 2003: 81). These motifs have been singled out for they are very "powerful, primordial patterns—archetypes—that can lead to creations of universal symbols, characters, stories, and myths" (*ibid.*). How this tale type grew out of heterogeneous cultures is a matter of great mystery till today. However, a Jungian interpretation of the archetypes will give a clue to this problem; for the archetypes are a clue to the mysterious birth of similar human mental patterns and experiences in diverse and heterogeneous cultures the world over. We therefore firmly believe in the unity in diversity. In this context, what Andrew Lang says deserves our attention: "we know that similar patterns, similar art . . . have thus been independently evolved; so have similar cosmic myths, similar fables, similar riddles, similar proverbs, similar customs and institutions" (Lang 1893: xv).

It will sound rather fascinating if we also know something about the distinctive cultural identity of the Meiteis as reflected in the tale *Sandrembi Chaisra.* These will constitute the local variants or motifs:

1. The existence of co-wives expresses the polygamous family structure in the Meitei community (now not as widespread as earlier). Hostility, jealousy, malevolent activities of the co-wives were part of such family structure. Stepmothers are infamously known for their cruelty often unleashed on the senior wife's children in Manipuri tales. Since olden times (and still today in the villages) fishing has remained a chief means of livelihood for the Meiteis. The two mothers of Sandrembi and Chaisra go fishing.
2. The Meitei people believe in the rebirth or transmigration of the human soul. We find in the tale many transformations. Repeated deaths followed by repeated births or transformations are seen, from human being to tortoise, bird, fruit tree and so on.
3. Number seven is believed to be very auspicious in Manipuri culture. Sandrembi keeps the tortoise hidden in a water pot so that on the seventh day it would turn into a human being; Sandrembi is asked by her dead mother in her dream again to keep the wrapped up bones of the tortoise for seven days but she violated the interdiction. Again the king keeps the bird so that it would turn into the earlier queen on the seventh day. The gardener keeps the fruit to eat but he forgets for seven days so the fruit turns into the original queen.
4. The tale chronicles fetching water by girls which in the past was an important scene of meeting between romantic young men and girls. Rivers, lakes, and ponds became romantic spots in the pastoral rural life. Fishing in the lakes individually or communally was also a long tradition amongst the Meiteis.

5. Marriage by kidnapping or abduction of the girl by a young man was very common in the Meitei community. In the myth *Konthoujam Lairembi* the sky god Sorarel abducts Tamphaleima who later on becomes a goddess. In the tale the king on horseback comes and abducts Sandrembi and makes her his queen.
6. Invitation of married girls to feast at their parents' home is a living tradition among the Meiteis. Sandrembi is invited by her stepmother and stepsister to a feast and is killed by pouring hot water.
7. The sword fight between Sandrembi and Chaisra is in keeping with the heroic tradition of the Meiteis and their martial art, which at crucial moments was used as a means of dispensing justice.

Such local variants are a distinctive cultural character in the tale, and they are to demonstrate the tradition to which the tale belongs. Anna Birgitta Rooth remarks: "Thus a motif may not be detached from its connections in order to be used for comparative studies. First and foremost a motif must be seen in connection with the variant it belongs to; and this variant must be seen in connection with the tradition within the area concerned" (152). Further Rooth goes on to emphasize one of the ideas central to folklore research that while collecting folkloric materials the local and regional traits, or motifs are not to be altered for they determine the identity of the culture of the people to which such elements belong. She found such local variants when she collected more than seven hundred Cinderella tales and the differences are interesting ingredients of the tales for comparative analysis.

In my study of Manipuri Cinderella *Sandrembi Chaisra* what is universal or global constitutes the common motifs available in the Cinderella tales and what is local is the variants rooted in the specific local culture and traditions. Cultural differences give birth to variants. Consider the remark: "Whereas the fish or turtle as helper is found in those variants which appear to represent a tradition which is purely Indian, the motif of the cow or goat occurs in variants which contain motifs common to those Near Eastern or European variants" (*ibid.* 199). Evidently transformation into a tortoise after death in *Sandrembi Chaisra* is characteristically oriental. Similarly, certain common motifs found in the oriental Cinderella are the killing of the heroine and her repeated transformations until she returns to her earlier human form. Such motifs are rarely found in the European versions of Cinderella. Cruelty and oppression of stepmother and step-sister are universal in Cinderella type tales. Method of oppression is also mainly in the nature of inflicting pain—using coercive measures, forcing or subjecting one to hard domestic chores, restrictions imposed on others, and in extreme cases even death occurs. The motif of "the dead mother as the helper" appears two times in the dream of Sandrembi; and "the spying motif" is also present when Chaisra stealthily peeps at the tortoise kept hidden by Sandrembi.

From the above study it may be ascertained that *Sandrembi Chaisra* is a blend of AT 510A Cinderella + AT 408 The Three Oranges. It is enigmatic to find how these internationally known motifs are present in such a tale such that the striking similarities are as interesting as the differences. Both elements generate fruitful inquiry into the nature of the growth and prevalence of this tale type. In folklore research such dissimilarities and motif variants are considered unique qualities of specific cultures or what we may call local variants. Bascom in his study of a Hausa tale thus argues: "Despite its omissions, despite its very different conclusion, and despite its presumably African accretions, such as the vomiting frog, this to me is clearly a Cinderella tale" (153). Many people hold the view that stories were traded, diffused from one place to another during peace and war. Stotter argues: "Certainly stories do cross borders, as indicated by the similar themes and tales that have been collected in diverse cultures" (15). While at the same time the universal working of human mind in similar conditions creating similar patterns, images and archetypes as an evolutionary process is also understood as vital towards analyzing the growth of the same motifs in tales simultaneously or at varying periods of time in many parts of the world. No single approach or observation on such a problem is absolute. The extent of the theory that tales travelled across borders of nations and continents may sound too credulous to believe. We have to make use of history, anthropology, ethnography and psychology in relation to cosmic rhythms and patterns to interpret and explore every aspect of a tale or a myth.

Works Cited

Aarne, Antti and Stith Thompson. 1961. *The Types of the Folktale*. Helsinki: Suomalainen Tiedeakatemia Academia Scientiarum Fennica. FFCommunication No. 184, 1987.

Aung, Maung Htin. *Folktales of Burma.* New Delhi: Sterling, 2nd ed., 1980.

Bascom, William R. *Contribution to Folkloristics*. Meerut: Archana, 1981.

Dundes, Alan. *Cinderella: A Casebook.* Wisconsin: U of Wisconsin P, 1988.

Goswami, Praphulladatta. 1960. *Ballads and Tales of Assam*. Guwahati: U of Guwahati, 1970.

Hartland, E. Sidney. Notes on Cinderella. Alan Dundes, ed. *Cinderella: A Casebook.* Wisconsin: The U of Wisconsin P., 1888.

Lang, Andrew. Introduction. *Cinderella* by Marian Roalfe Cox. London: The Folklore Society, 1893.

Lule, Jack. Waters of Death in Central Africa. Kwadwo Anokwa *et al. Mass Communication.* New Delhi: Cengage Learning, 2003.

Rooth, Anna-Birgitta. *The Cinderella Cycle*. Lund: C.W.K. Gleerup, 1951.

Stotter, Ruth. *About Story: Writings on Stories and Storytelling 1980-1994*. London: Stotter Press, 1994.

Thompson, Stith. 1946. *The Folktale*. Los Angeles: U of California P, 1977.

Ting, Nai-Tung. *The Cinderella Cycle: In China and Indo China*. Helsinki: FF Communications, No. 213, 1974.

Goddess Temples in North-Eastern India: Overcoming Narrative Distance in Place-Lore

ÜLO VALK
University of Tartu

This article about the power of imagination in religious traditions comes from Tartu, a university town at a long distance from north-eastern India. It is winter outside. Streets, roofs and trees are covered with snow, the Emajõgi River is frozen and daylight is a limited resource. However, as my mind is wandering in Assam, I can visualize the flow of the mighty Brahmaputra and light green paddy fields in valley. Next, I am strolling in the sunny streets of Guwahati and then rising up the ancient stone stairs on Nīlāchal hill, approaching the Kāmākhyā temple. Imagination can cover long distances in a moment, evoke memories of the past and bring to life fantasy worlds full of colours and sensations. This article explores some vernacular myths of Assam that have a close connection with landscapes, temples and significant places. In some cases this storyworld of deities and supernatural events frames and pervades the whole daily environment of the people who carry the mythic knowledge. Places bear visual marks of the deeds of gods and through these traces, the presence of otherworldly (*aloukik*) realm becomes manifest. Through narratives and narrating this mysterious era is brought to life time and again, the mythic time-space is both present and continuous. Powerful deities such as Śiva, Parvatī, Kāmākhyā and others appear as embodied characters who live on earth and participate in worldly activities. Christopher J. Fuller has noted that great Hindu gods "with powers over the cosmos, are normally thought to distance themselves from mundane problems affecting ordinary people" (36). However, in some places the almighty deities maintain close connection with the life-world through tangible material reality. How does it happen that some locations are marked off as extraordinary, sacred places, distinctly different from their mundane surroundings? How can people in their daily lives access the transcendent mythic realities? In this article I argue that deities are evoked through the art of storytelling and their sensible presence becomes possible through certain vernacular genres. I also claim that these generic qualities of certain narratives make people travel and seek the experience of the mythic realm.

The genre of myth has been widely discussed and theorized from a variety of angles, including social, psychological, literary, structural, performative, religious, ritual, ideological and political ones (e.g. Lincoln, Doty, Csapo, Siikala). The history of mythological research is long and myth has multiple definitions. In this article, I understand myths as grand narratives, monumental stories that have strong and lasting impact on the lives of communities. They bind groups together as makers and markers of their identity. Thus, the story about God, who creates the world within six days and makes mankind in his own image, links all generations of Christians on all continents. The narrative about a great sage, who achieved the ultimate knowledge about the causes of suffering, fought a cosmic battle against the grand demon Māra and preached the doctrine of Four Noble Truths, is shared by all Buddhists. The time-space of myths tends to be separated from contemporary world, as it is both transcendent and distant, and not bound to the laws of nature as we know them. Myths are full of wonderworks, cosmic dramas and extraordinary feats. Mythic acts of deities usually have no human witnesses but they are well documented in multiple sources, in ancient literary works, in holy scripts and in the endless course of oral storytelling. It is the very tradition of transmitting myths from generation to generation that links us to the primordial time of creation. Thus, the famous treatise of ancient India *Bṛhadāraṇyaka Upaniṣad* lists long lines of teachers who have transmitted the philosophical and mythical wisdom, leading finally to the divine realm—to the deities Vāc ('speech'), Āditya (interpreted as the Sun), and finally to the demiurgic deity Prajā-pati and the great Creator Brahmā himself as the source of ultimate knowledge (VI.5.1-4; Radhakrishnan 331-33). However, the uninterrupted line of transmission not only provides connection with the remote past, but also emphasizes our temporary distance from the beginning. The divine realm is far away and seems inaccessible to us, mortals who are bound to physical bodies and mundane realities.

One of the fundamental principles of folkloristic genre systems is the distinction that is made between true stories and those that are fabulated for artistic purposes. It is not easy to determine the relationship between social and historical realities on the one hand and the imaginary realm on the other hand as even most fantastic stories can express truths and values that are of utmost importance for the communities. One of the problems of understanding myths lies in the fact that they are remarkably detached from the world as we perceive it in their fabulous images and extraordinary events but they are told as true stories to be taken seriously—even in our age of prevailing rationalism. This paradox can be addressed through analyzing different levels of spatial and temporal distance as they appear in the storyworld. Kaarina Koski in her article on Finnish belief narratives has characterized these levels, starting from the reflection of social reality as it is. When beliefs about the supernatural are transmitted, they often appear as non-narrative utterances, but even when they are expressed in narrative form, the stories can be realistic and close to reality. Secondly, narrative events can be "framed to a certain time and space" and "located in the nearby surroundings but in a moment and place in which the balance between the inside and outside worlds has been disrupted" (Koski 343-44). These stories are dramatic, expressing the conflict between humans and the other world, and the element of supernatural in them is remarkable. However, the plots are located into nearby storyworld,[1] which is not detached from the life-world; the narrated extraordinary events and social reality coalesce to a great extent. When the distance between social reality and storyworld is maximized, the fantastic elements preponderate and we can talk about an ontologically different, distant storyworld. (*Ibid.* 344-45) Myths clearly are a member of the latter category but they include characters who are of vital importance to the storytellers and their audiences—the deities, whose partnership with individuals and communities is crucial, especially in the time of crises. Contact with deities can be achieved through prayers, rituals and other religious practices. The realm of mythic events is evoked through storytelling as a faraway reality, however, storytelling also provides means to minimize this distance and present the divine as part of here and now. Moreover, narratives produce evidence to confirm the veracity of the fantastic events. How?

The imagined mythic world often appears as a nearby reality around us, it is physically close as the venues of marvellous events of the past are still present, and their traces are visible in the landscape. Diana L. Eck has characterized India as a living, storied and intricately connected landscape, constructed on the presupposition of divine plurality and plenitude (2-5). One of the grand narratives that ties India together is the myth about the marriage of Śiva and goddess Satī, her tragic suicide, and dismemberment of her dead body into multiple parts that fall all over the country (see e.g. Courtright; Eck 195-97). These places are known as *śakta pithā*s—places of divine power of the Goddess where she is constantly living. *Kālikā Purāna*, a classical text in Sanskrit that dates from tenth-eleventh centuries, and originates from Assam, lists the following *śakta pithā*s:

> First of all the pair of feet (of Satī) fell at Devīkūṭa, thereafter the pair of thighs, for the welfare of the world, fell at Uddīyāna and then the female pudenda fell on the mountain, named Kāmagiri in Kāmarūpa, the navel also fell there on the ground of that mountain, the pair of breasts, adorned with golden chain, fell at Jālandhara, the arms along with the neck fell on the mountain named Pūrṇagiri and then the head fell beyond the region of Kāmarūpa. (18, 41-43)

According to Dines Ch. Sircar, the passage above mentions localities in contemporary West Bengal (Devīkūṭa), Pakistan (Uddīyāna), Punjab (Jālandhara), and somewhere in the South (Pūrṇagiri) (17-18). Kāmagiri mountain, the site of *yoni*, is traditionally identified as Nīlāchal hill with the famous goddess Kāmākhyā temple. Located in Guwahati in Assam, this place is a great pilgrimmage centre and site of many-sided ritual and devotional activities (Dold). The site at the foothill, mentioned in *Kālikā Purāna,* where the navel of goddess fell, is Ugratārā temple in Guwahati city.

The divine body of Goddess thus merges with places in landscape that continuously radiate *śakti* and attract worshippers seeking direct contact with the divine. Comparative research on sacred sites in world religions has shown that their 'sacredness' is often marked by certain salient features, such as "holes and openings in the ground, cracks between rocks, and caves" (Anttonen 297). Kāmākhyā temple on Nīlāchal hill fits well with this characteristics: instead of a man-made image (*mūrti*), the *yoni* of Goddess is there worshipped in the form of a natural spring that flows out from a cavity in the rock. Whereas Kāmākhyā temple hides one of the most famous *śakta pithā*s in India, Assam is rich in other goddess shrines that are connected with the same origin myth about the dismemberment of Satī's body. Whereas the classical number of *śakta pithā*s in pan-Indian traditions is usually 51 or 108 (Eck 287), the actual number is infinite because folkloric variation constantly generates new places that are affiliated to the basic myth.

My field trips in Assam have led me to several temples, where the priests, wandering sadhus and other people who carry the vernacular knowledge, have explained the origin of temple in connection with the mythic dismemberment of Satī's body. Thus, just like the Ugratārā temple in Guwahati, the ancient Naagshankar (Śiva) temple in Jamuguri, Sonitpur district has been built to mark the place where Satī's navel has fallen. The ancient Hatimura temple at Silghat in Nagaon district is dedicated to goddess Durgā and houses her grand stone image. This place acquired its power when Satī's right hand fell there, as it was explained by the Nepalese sadhu who maintains the temple (my fieldwork notes from February 2011). During the same field trip my late folklorist friend Kailash Dutta showed me his fieldwork area among the ethnic group of Thengal Kacharis. We visited a small Durgā shrine (*than*) that had been established in 1942 in Duliagaon village near Narayanpur. There is no Brahmin to take care of this shrine that is managed by Mr. Dulal Neog who has taken over this duty from his father. As he told us, during the *Durgā Pūjā* celebrations he performs animal sacrifices, dances ecstatically and predicts the future to the villagers. During these performances he becomes possessed, as the Goddess takes over his body and speaks through him. According to his words, Satī's tongue must have fallen into the location of the shrine. How else to explain his amazing eloquence and long monologues that he cannot remember after the state of possession is over? Thus, the myth about dismemberment of the Goddess is very much alive and finds expression in endless storytelling. Some stories are well established in tradition, others are emergent. We can see that the narrative distance to mythic realities can be overcome if the nearby environment appears as the stage of grand events of the past. Mythic characters can also be internalized in the state of possession, when medium acquires the divine power of verbal expression. The divine realm of great deities thus becomes immanent in the physical world and appears as a lived reality.

Many temple legends in Assam tell about discontinuities and ruptures in history. Stories claim that shrines have been destroyed, rituals have stopped, and the place has fallen into oblivion. However, temples are rediscovered and restored, thanks to the activities of outstanding historical persons, such as great kings. Sometimes the goddess herself appears and reveals the forgotten place of worship. *Kālikā Purāna* tells about the king Naraka, the first mythical ruler of Assam (Kāmarūpa) who invaded the country and conquered the ancient Prāg-jyotiṣa kingdom. He was commanded by his father Viṣṇu not to worship any other deity except the local goddess Kāmākhyā (Kakati 13-14). According to the mythic tradition, the original magnificent goddess temple on Nīlāchal hill had been constructed by the love deity Kāmadeva with the help of the artisan god Viśvakarma. The initiative had come from Śiva himself who had told Kāmadeva to erect the temple. In return Śiva restored his former grace and beauty that had been damaged by Śiva's burning anger (Sarma 2002: 4). In a small booklet, sold in little shops on Nīlāchal hill for pilgrims and tourists, Ganga Sarma describes the original construction of the temple and its decline as follows: "The temple was full of architectural and sculptural beauties. Even to-day one can find the beautiful images of sixty four yoginies and eighteen images of Bhairavas. Perhaps due to some upheaval against religion or natural calamities, the upper part of the temple was ravaged and the lower part was gradually submerged." (*Ibid.* 13) Contemporary residents of Nīlāchal hill can show stone blocks, bas-reliefs, sculptures and other elements of the original stone temple, which had been constructed by deities. The stone statue of the builder, artisan god Viśvakarma riding an elephant, is nowadays standing behind the temple.[2] Construction of other parts of the pre-historic shrine, such as the stone staircases that lead to the temple, have been attributed to the mythic ruler Naraka.

Long after the mythic establishment of the temple and its glorious early history, the site at Nīlāchal hill was rediscovered by the king Biswasingha and his brother (Devsharma, Sarma 2002). As the story goes, they meet an old woman in the jungle who offers water to them and tells that the mound is a form of a mighty goddess who can fulfil all desires. She instructs the two men how to worship the goddess with sacrifices, valuable clothes and ornaments. With the help of goddess, the king Biswasingha establishes peace in his country and promises to build a new, golden temple. On the order of the king the forested place, inhabited by wild animals, is cleaned, and excavations reveal the original stone temple, that had been built by Kāmadeva. A new brick temple is constructed on top of the ancient temple site but mysteriously, the new construction collapses several times. Then the goddess appears to the king as a maiden, sits on his bed at night and reminds him of his earlier promise to build a golden temple. The frightened king asks her forgiveness and the merciful goddess tells him that if he does not have enough gold to construct the whole temple, it would be sufficient to add a piece of gold to each brick. Following this advice the construction of the temple is completed (Devsharma 38-43; Sarma 13-15). There is no historical evidence about reconstruction of the temple during the reign of Biswasingha (1520-1540), who was the first king of the Koch dynasty. Chronicles claim that his successor Naranārāyaṇa (1540-1580) restored the temple in 1565 and revived the worship of goddess Kāmākhyā (Sarma, Borah 21-22). Pilgrims and other people who crowd the premises of the temple are well aware of the mythic history of the place, starting from Śiva, Satī and the emergence of the *śakti pīth*, followed by the construction of the original temple by Kāmadeva and Viśvakarma, and its reconstruction by local rulers. Knowledge about the past grandeur of the Kāmākhyā shrine on Nīlāchal hill attracts people from near and afar and visiting the place is like a finalization of the story in the live experience of being there.

There are several other, less famous Kāmākhyā temples in Assam. One of them is in Silghat on the southern bank of Brahmaputra in Nagaon district, about twenty kilometres from Tezpur. Located in picturesque landscape, this active and freshly renovated temple draws many people, some of whom come to the popular picnic place on the Brahmaputra River but they also pay a visit to the goddess. This temple has three ancient stone idols (*mūrti*) of deities: Ganeśa outside, in front of the entrance, and Durgā and Kāmākhyā inside the main shrine, standing next to each other. Different from the temple on Nīlāchal hill here the devotees can meet the goddess Kāmākhyā face to face as she is carved in stone.

On 22 January 2012, I visited the temple with Kailash Dutta and Parag Moni Sarma, folklorists from Tezpur University. We interviewed the Brahmin Tarun Barthakur who told us the main episodes in the history of the shrine, starting from the marriage of Śiva and Pārvatī, who had selected this place, known as Kāmkut or Kāmgiri hill, to spend their wedding night. Afterwards they visited the holy site on Nīlāchal hill, where Pārvatī appeared as Kāmākhyā and showed this new form to other deities. The artisan deity Viśvakarma, using her as a model, crafted the stone image of goddess. As Tarun Barthakur told us, devotees at Nīlāchal hill had started to worship this image instead of the *yoni*, which had been placed there by Śiva himself. Deities discussed the matter and decided that it would be better to shift the *mūrti* to another place. Therefore a dream was revealed to Vānamaldev, a king of Sālasthambha dynasty who reigned in Tezpur. According to the dream he had to move the stone image of Kāmākhyā away from the original location, and he brought it to Kāmkut at Silghat. He also constructed the stone temple to mark the place where Śiva and Pārvatī had spent their wedding night. Tarun Barthakur obviously had much practice in telling the stories to visitors and he knew a lot of details about the history of the temple. Below is the summary of his talk.

> Centuries passed and the year was 1745.[3] Then the Ahom King Pramatta Singha was travelling up the river, coming from Guwahati. It turned dark and he stopped to stay nearby in the place called Gosanighat. At night, the goddess appeared in his dream as an old woman and revealed to him the temple site. The next day he spoke of his dream to his fellow men and asked them to go to the hill and look around, and then tell him what they could see there. They returned, and said that they had seen a stone temple there. The place was clean and beautiful, but there was not a single human being there. The King took a bath and went to see the temple with his fellow men. He went up to Kāmgiri hillock and met the old woman who he had seen in his dream. He told his fellows that he had seen this old woman in his dream. Then he asked her: "Who are you?" And the old woman said that she had already introduced herself in the dream. The King agreed that he had heard her voice in the dream. The old woman told him that in the past Hara [Śiva] and Pārvatī had met here and that the stone idol had been brought here. The King realized that this was the idol of Kāmākhyā which had been brought from the Guwahati Kāmākhyā temple. The old woman invited him to come and see the image of Kāmākhyā. She asked the King to rebuild the temple. The King told her about the hardships he endured in ruling the kingdom. The woman said that all the problems would be solved if he would build the new temple. "You don't have a son, but you will gain one. I'll be there to protect you from the attacks of enemies." The woman entered the temple and the King followed her. She disappeared in the darkness, but the *mūrti* was there. He could not find the woman anywhere and the King realized that he had met Kāmākhyā. Then he decided to build the temple and he brought a priest from Kāmākhyā temple. This was Tarun Barthakur's ancestor Lambudar—a famous priest who had seen the Goddess. The King also brought two other Brahmin families and made them responsible for looking after the temple. He also brought some other families to work for the temple

> and thus the adjacent Kāmākhyā village was formed. It has been connected with the temple for a long time.

The story starts from the mythical age of *satya-yuga*, when Śiva lost his first wife and met her again, when she was reborn as Pārvatī. The site of the temple is intimately connected with the biography of the divine couple and is marked off as the hill of passion (Kāmgiri). Next, the stone image of Kāmākhyā is identified as an artwork of god Viśvakarma who had also built the original goddess temple at Nīlāchal hill. Its translocation to the current place is explained as the intervention of Vānamaldev, a historical king who got a revelation in the dream. This king had also founded the original temple at Silghat which had been abandoned, until centuries later another historical king, Pramatta Singha (1744-1751) discovered it through his dream. According to the instructions of Kāmākhyā herself he restores the temple, establishes the adjacent village, settles there three Brahminic families and restarts the uninterrupted worship that continues until now. The mythic storyworld thus offers the scenery for the current temple, which is located on the hillock, where Śiva and Pārvatī spent their wedding night, and which houses the marvellous stone image, crafted by the artisan deity Viśvakarma, depicting the Goddess Kāmākhyā as she appeared in bodily form. The Brahmin families who serve in the temple today represent the historical lineage, and thus lead to the great events of the past. In this way, the narrative distance between the mythic realm and lived reality is diminished.

What gives power to certain places, such as the goddess temples, to attract people, pilgrims and other visitors and make them move, sometimes over long distances? It has been argued in tourist studies that the primary motivation of tourists is the pursuit of 'authenticity' (Wearing 29). Travellers are looking for something unusual, for extraordinary experiences, for existential authenticity: "a potential existential state of Being which is to be activated by tourist activities" (Wang 352). Obviously, storytelling has a great role to play in preparing minds of the people to these ultimate experiences. The more they know about the place before the visit, the more nuanced can their impressions become. As people are visiting sacred sites away from their homes, they are travelling two distances—both in the geographical and narrative space. They are also travelling back in time, as their imagination leads them to the primeval events when deities were active on earth. These travellers experience a liminal world of in-betweenness—both tangibly nearby, physically present, and elusively dreamlike, emergent in storytelling and easily fading away. Through the power of imagination these mythical realms come into being, and through the power of storytelling these worlds are in constant making, and can be created time and again. Place-lore is thus a passage to the otherworldly reality. The aura of authenticity is not tied to places only, it can also be evoked through narratives and memories. Places can be experienced through stories and vice versa. Whatever the starting point is, the narrative distance between lived reality and the mythic realm is not absolute but can be overcome.

NOTES

1. Kaarina Koski uses the term Taleworld, following the work of Katherine Young who distinguished between Storyrealm (situation of narrating) and Taleworld (the narrative realm) (Young 1987). In this article however, I use the term "storyworld" to refer to the world as it is evoked by a narrative, both implicitly and explicitly (Herman 106).
2. The stone sculpture depicts a deity riding an elephant. Iconographically, the image could also represent Indra, not Viśvakarma. It is equally likely that the stone image in the Kāmākhyā temple in Silghat historically represents Kālī, not Kāmākhyā. However, in the vernacular imagination these *mūrti*s belong to a certain storyworld and this context (re)defines their identity.

3. According to the Assamese chronology, the year was 1667.

Bibliography

Anttonen, Veikko. 2003. 'Sacred Sites as Markers of Difference: Exploring Cognitive Foundations of Territoriality,' *Dynamics of Tradition: Perspectives on Oral Poetry and Folk Belief*, ed. Lotte Tarkka. Studia Fennica Folkloristica 13. Helsinki: Finnish Literature Society. 291-305.

Courtright, Paul B. 2011. 'Searching for Satī,' *Studying Hinduism in Practice*, ed. Hillary P. Rodrigues, 37-45.

Csapo, Eric 2005. *Theories of Mythology*. Malden, Oxford, Victoria, Blackwell.

Dold, Patricia A. 2011. 'Pilgrimmage to Kāmākhyā through text and lived religion: Some forms of the Goddess at Assamese temple site,' *Studying Hinduism in Practice*, ed. Hillary Rodrigues, 46-61.

Doty, William G. 2000. *Mythography: The Study of Myths and Rituals*. Tuscaloosa: The University of Alabama Press.

Eck, Diana L. 2012. *India: a Sacred Geography*. New York: Harmony Books.

Fuller, Christopher John. 1992. *The Camphor Flame. Popular Hinduism and Society in India*. Princeton: Princeton University Press.

Herman, David. 2009. *Basic Elements of Narrative*. Chichester: Wiley-Blackwell.

Rodrigues, Hillary P. *Studying Hinduism in Practice*. London and New York: Routledge.

Kakati, Banikanta. 1989. *The Mother Goddess Kamakhya*. Guwahati: Publication Board Assam.

Kālikā Purāna = The Kālikāpurāṇa (Text, Introduction & Translation in English). B.N. Shastri. I-III. Delhi: Nag, 1991-1992.

Koski, Kaarina. 2008. 'Narrative Time-Spaces in Belief Legends,' *Space and Time in Europe: East and West, Past and Present*, ed. Mirjam Mencej. Ljubljana: University of Ljubljana Press. 337-53.

Lincoln, Bruce. 1999. *Theorizing Myth: Narrative, Ideology and Scholarship*. Chicago: The University of Chicago Press.

Radhakrishnan S. 1996. *The Principal Upaniṣads*, ed. with Introduction, Text, Translation and Notes. New Delhi: HarperCollins, 1953.

Sarma, Ganga. 2002. *Kamrup Kamakhya*. Guwahati: Bishnu Prakashan.

Sarma, Pradip and Bosanta Borah. 2010. 'Facts from History,' *Heritage of Kāmākhyā on the Nīlāchala Hill*, ed. G.N. Bhuyan, Sujatha Nayak. Guwahati: Vivekananda Kendra Institute of Culture. 20-28.

Siikala, Anna-Leena. 2012. 'Myths as Multivalent Poetry: Three Complementary Approaches,' *Mythic Discourses: Studies in Uralic Traditions*, ed. Frog, Anna-Leena Siikala & Eila Stepanova. Studia Fennica Folkloristica 20. Helsinki: Finnish Literature Society. 17-39.

Sircar, D.C. 1973; 2004. *The Śākta Pīṭhas*. Delhi: Motilal Banarsidas.

Urban, Hugh B. 2011. *The Power of Tantra. Religion, Sexuality and the Politics of South Asian Studies*. London, New York: I.B. Tauris.

Wang, Ning. 1999. 'Rethinking Authenticity in Tourism Experience.' *Annals of Tourism Research*. 26: 2. 349-70.

Wearing, Stephen; Stevenson, Deborah; Young Tamara. 2010. *Tourist Cultures: Identity, Place and the Traveller*. Los Angeles, London, New Delhi, Singapore, Washington DC: Sage.

Young, Katherine. 1978. *Taleworlds and Storyrealms: The Phenomenology of Narrative*. Martinus Nijhoff: Dordrecht.

Acknowledgement

This research has been supported by the Estonian Ministry of Education and Research (Institutional Research Grant 2-43).

Oral History and Storytelling: Perspectives of the Chakmas

PANKAJ ROY
Government Kamalanagar College, Chawngte, Mizoram

Storytelling may be broadly defined as an ancient method of conveying ideas, intimations, and emotions in a narrative form with or without the accompaniment of music or visual art. Originally storytelling, an aspect of oral tradition, has evolved from its earliest form to the modern period with the inclusion of a variety of multimedia applications. Folklorists generally do not approve of such inclusive definitions. In her scholarly analysis of the history of storytelling, *The World of Storytelling* (1990), Anne Pellowski defines storytelling: "The art or craft of narration of stories in verse and/ or prose, as performed or led by one person before a live audience; the stories narrated may be spoken, chanted, or sung, with or without musical, pictorial, and/ or other accompaniment and may be learned from oral, printed, or mechanically recorded sources; one of its purposes may be that of entertainment" (15).

What is the purpose of storytelling then? Pellowski, in line with other theorists, says that storytelling may have started as informal entertainment or play, and only gradually became intertwined with religious rituals, historical recitations, and educational functions. Most theorists suggest that storytelling fulfils the desire for playacting and meets entertainment needs while helping to explain the surrounding physical world or helping honour or placate the supernatural force(s) believed to be present in the world. Storytelling can help explain and express strong emotions and experiences in memorable, long-lasting ways through the intricate use of rhythm, rhyme, and repetition. Storytelling can help preserve traditions, customs, and societal standards, while bestowing immortality on leaders or ancestors. Pellowski notes the earliest evidence of storytelling may be found in the Westcar Papyrus of the Egyptians, which includes tales of encounters between a pyramid builder named Khufu or Cheops and his sons. One of the most famous tales recorded on papyrus is known as 'The Shipwrecked Sailor.' Pellowski traces the development of the Bardic tradition, defining the bard as, "a storyteller whose function is to create and/ or perform poetic oral narrations that chronicle events or praise the illustrious forebears and present leaders of a tribal, cultural, or national group" (21). The bard was a storyteller, a poet, and a musician. The term bard had its introduction through Greek and Roman tales of the Celts. Bards have also been known as rhapsodes, minstrels, or jongleurs.

In such a situation where lies the missing link between folk, tradition, society and history? Paul Thompson has said "All history depends ultimately upon its social purpose. This is why in the past it has been handed down by oral tradition and written chronicle." Sometimes the social purpose of history is obscure: academics who pursue fact-finding research on remote problems as that of the Chakma history without attempting to relate their discoveries to any more general interpretations, insisting on the technical virtue of scholarship and pursuit of knowledge for its own sake, are merely concerned to protect their own professional interests and offer no challenge to the social system. The challenge to oral history vis-à-vis storytelling lies partly in relation to this essential social purpose of history. This is a major reason why it has excited some historians and frightened others. It can be used as a means to transform both the content and purpose of history, to change the focus of history, open up new areas of inquiry, can break down barriers between generation and world outside.

Many world folk epics from a variety of cultures have been preserved because of storytelling traditions. Some examples are: *Beowulf*, an Anglo-Saxon epic of courage in the face of brute strength; *Gilgamesh*, a Sumerian epic of the Sumerian king, Gilgamesh, and his friendship with Enkidu, the half-beast, half-man being created to destroy him; the *Iliad*, a Greek epic of the Trojan War; the *Odyssey*, depicting Odysseus on his homeward journey from Troy; *Story of Sigurd* (Siegfried), a Norse legend; the *Volsunga Saga*, the adventures of Sigurd, including the killing of a dragon named Fafnir; *The Merry Adventures of Robin Hood and King Arthur and His Knights*, legendary English tales of daring and bravery; *Song of Roland*, the French epic; *Sundiata, The Epic of the Lion King*, a legendary African tale of how Sundiata became King of Mali; *The Tain*, an Irish tale of the legendary hero Cuchulain, his birth, battles and ultimate death; the *Ramayana* of India, often relayed in the form of *Ramlila, Raslila, Nautanki* and the *Gengkhuli* of the Chakmas. This last one through the art of storytelling runs live for weeks, some sort of crude ballad sung by a single singer nonstop and retelling the traditions and life of great conquerors and general folk alike. It reflects upon both the village and urban life of the mass and includes an element of connectedness between the past and the present. If these were prevalent once, then how and through what stages oral history lost its original eminence? If we look at the scope of oral traditions in pre-literate societies, we can find one. At that stage all history was oral and everything had to be remembered, from crafts to seasons, to laws and transactions. Jan Vansina in his classic *Oral Traditions: A study in historical methodology* (1965) divides African Traditions into five categories and all of them are oral in nature and the social importance of these traditions lies in handing them down from generation to generation with minimum distortion. Practices as group testimony on ritual occasions, disputations, schools for teaching traditional lore, recitations on taking office could preserve exact tests through the centuries, including archaisms even after they had ceased to be understood. In Rwanda, for example, genealogists or *abacurabwenge* had to remember the names of kings and queens, memorialists or *abateekeerzi* had to know the important events of various reigns, rhapsodists or *abasizi* preserved the panegyrics on the kings and *abiiru* keeping the secrets of the dynasties. Each of them was responsible for the preservation of different types of tradition. Another instance of village tradition bearers can be found in Alex Haley's *Roots* (1976), in which the author rediscovers his own ancestry through a *griot* or tradition-bearer of his clan and his clan name, *Kinte*. Nevertheless Haley's search brings home with rare power the *standing* of the oral historian before the spread of documentation in literate societies made redundant such public moments of historical revelation. Many documents of the past in the public domain are passed on to the present generation as authoritative private documents, and even those rituals, names, songs, stories from memories stand as the final authority and the guarantee of transmission to the future.

The Chakma society is very rich in oral traditions and notable among them are the ballads of *Gyangkulee Gheet* which not only gives entertainment but also narrates the Chakma life of the past. These ballads are sung by the ballad singers called *Gyangkullya* who are trained and specialized in this field. The art of singing can be learnt from two sources: (1) Manei Sikkya where the *Gyangkullya* is trained by a Guru singer and (2) Deva Sikkya where the *Gyangkullya* is trained in dreams by spirits. The *Gyangkullya* holds a respectable position in the Chakma society. He does not sing anywhere and at any moment except on special invitation called *Fang* and with a simple ritual. There are more than 13 *Palhas* (parts) narrating different accounts. They are *Lokhi Palha, Sargha Palha, Sadeng Giri Palha, Sritti Pathan*

Palha, Kuki Dhara Palha, Radhansha Palha; Radhamohn-Dhanpudi Palha, Chadigang Chara Palha, Geelapara Palha, Ranyabera Palha, Kameshdhan-Narpudi Palha, Phul Para Palha,and Lorbho-Midhungi Palha.

It is not possible to ascertain the exact period of composition of each of the *Palhas*. On the basis of the genealogy of the Chakma kings and other aspects as narrated from ancient time till date, it is assumed that these *palhas* have been updated from time to time. However, it is certain that these *palhas* were initially composed after the *Angarkul Roang* (Arakan) expedition by King Bijoygiri from Kalabaga. There are different periods and dates assigned to the expedition of Bijoygiri. He led Arakan expedition in 590; but according to Jeevansar Bikkhu, Bijoygiri led expedition in 595, and again according to Suprasanna Banarjee, Bijoygiri annexed Arakan after defeating Maghs in 994-95. But Pannalal Majumdar is of the view that Bijoygiri reigned from 615-645. There are other scholars who opine that Bijoygiri led expedition around 1192 and Lalsangliana, a Mizo scholar ascribed the date to 1600. It is interesting to note that a person, namely Suleiman Badshah appears in the *Radhamohn-Dhanpudi Palha* from whom the Magh Raja and the Kuki Raja sought help against the Chakmas. This Suleiman was a Persian trader who imported cowries from Maldives to Bengal around 850. Thus, from the above facts, the reign of Bijoygiri can be assigned to 9th century and probably *Radhamohn-Dhanpudi Palha* and the *Chadigang Chara Palha* were composed after this period. These ballads are purely oral in the Chakma language. The words in some of the *Palhas* especially in *Srittipattam palha* contain old Chakma archaic terms which are not in use today. The fact is that these *Palhas* are not sung frequently and hence it retains the old language which is a bit difficult to understand today. On the other hand, some of the *Palhas* like *Radhamohn-Dhanpudi Palha* and the *Chadigang Chara Palha* are sung frequently and hence it is mixed up with the modern Chakma language which is easy to understand.

The Chakmas keep *Pudhi*, *Vadya* has the literal meaning of physician and *Pudhi* means books. It is the physician's books dealing with medicines, their application, methods of treatment, history of different deities and their methods of worship, physical science, magical formulas, incantations, history of diseases and their symptoms, and so on. The Chakmas have been practising this *Vadyali* since long past. However, in modern days, this tradition lost its importance to some extent due to the advancement of modern medical treatment. It is said that these *Pudhis* were initially written on palm leaves and animal skins in the Chakma language and script but later copied on paper. The *Vadyali* has been taught by a *Guru Thagur* (teacher) to a *Shishya* (student). After training and when the *Guru* gains full confidence, the *Shishya* is allowed to practise independently. The *Vadya* initially indentifies the illness whether it is caused by *Manei Karam* (caused by human beings) or *Deva Karam* (caused by spirits) by touching *Nari* (nerves) of a patient or by applying other modes of examination. There are different methods of treatment viz. *Tallik* or *Daru* (application of medicines), *Mandar* (application of magic or incantation), *Tabit* application of talishman), *Pujo* (sacrificial worship) and *Kabi* or *Pudi Dena* (surgery). The Chakmas believe in external forces like ghosts, spirits, demons, deities, gods and goddesses and if the illness caused by these forces, the *Vadya* arranges *Pujo* to appease the deities and also applies *Daru* and *Mandar* and in other cases all the methods are applied except *Pujo* depending upon the diseases.

Another popular literature among the Chakmas is the *Gojenalama* written in the Chakma script and dialect by Shiv Charan, an ascetic. Here *Gojen* literally means creator or god and though the exact meaning of the term *Lama* is not known yet it may be part of the prayer (Bandana). Here, Shiv Charan prayed to various gods and goddesses, Saraswati, Chandra, Surjyo, tin Dev-Barma, Bishnu, Shiv; Saints, Guru (teacher), Mata-Pita (parents), etc. for wealth, beauty, son-daughter, money, chastity, education, abstinence from sin, all to conquer enemy and be in prosperity. The *Gojenalama* consisted of seven parts. It was written in 1184 B.E or 1777 A.D as it appeared in the main text. However, Tripur Chandra Sen assigned it as the Maghi Era (Burmese Era) because during this period Maghi Era was prevalent in the Chittagong region. Here is an extract from the last part of the *Gojenalama*:

> Sargapuri Berebong Singhasanat Bajibong
> Sonar Dulanat Dulibong Devar Bhangani Bhangibong
> Param Gojen Pujibong Sakal Dugottun Toribong
> Egaraso Surasi Bangla Lukero Ganane
> Boyara Loge Miji Gelung Mui Sib Charan Bhudbare.

There are more such scriptures which are oral as well as religious and medicinal in nature and are sung. So, it can be seen that the Chakmas used the oral form in absence of written documents and often in ballad form to pass it on to next generation, much like the Africans. It is a proven fact that these ballads also register the Chakma history and social nuances of the past. They point to the key social and political importance and provide a new basis for original projects, not just by professionals, but by students, by school children, and even by the people of the community as small as the Chakmas. For they don't have just to learn their own history, they can write it. Oral history gives history back to the people in their own words and in giving the past it also helps them produce a future of their own making.

Works Cited

Behra, Guru Charan. *Appropriating Folk Culture*. Delhi: Authorspress, 2008.

Chakma, Punyadhan. *Chakma Itihas*. Calcutta: ADSONS, 1982, p. 17.

Chakma, Jyotirmoy. 'A Brief Analysis of Chakma Folk Literatures and its Languages,' paper presented in Convention on Chakma Language organized by Sahitya Academy, North-East Centre for Oral Literature at Agartala, Tripura on 10-11 July 2010.

Dewan, Biraj Mohan. *Chakma Jatir miltibritta* (The History of Chakma Tribe). Rangamati: Sibali Art Press, 1969, p. 76.

Goody, Jack. *Myth, Ritual and the Oral*. New York: CUP, 2010.

Narayan, Kirin. *Story Tellers, Saints and Scoundrels: Folk Narrative in Hindu Religious Teaching*. Delhi: Motilal Banarasidas, 1992.

Pellowski, Anne. *The World of Storytelling*. Expanded and revised ed. New York: H.W. Wilson, 1990.

Mapping 'Arena Theatre': The Journey of 'Yatra' in Undivided Midnapore

SOUMYADEEP CHAKRABORTY
Research Scholar, Bankura University

Midnapore or Medinipur (undivided) as being a district not only acquires an important geo-political space in the topography of West Bengal but has also earned a unique and significant cultural space. The rich cultural baggage of Midnapore, a rural southern region of West Bengal, has amply been structured and contributed by several cultural genres and 'Yatra' is one of the most prominent among those. Yatra, which literally means a 'procession' or a 'journey,' is an important and integral part of the history and growth of the folk dramatic tradition in India. Yatra is basically a stylized folk form of drama that originated and was explored in different parts of Orissa and West Bengal with 'melodramatic performativity' and 'localized theatricality.' Ananda Lal, a renowned theatre-critic, remarks: "While going in a procession with a stylized dance-like walk to the rhythm of drums, they [actors] depict through simple gestures selected familiar episodes from the epic. From this processional theatre developed a style of arena theatre known as Yatra." (451)

Midnapore has not only contributed to these specificities of Yatra, it has laid significant mark on the development and dynamism of the genre. It is perhaps because of the mixed, intersectional cultural belonging of the residents of Midnapore that it has registered such prominent impression over this genre that originated from both Orissa and West Bengal. H.V. Bayley in his book *Memoranda of Midnapore* (1852) has complimented this afore-said issue by saying: "The people of Midnapore proper are generally composed of amalgamated race, who can neither be called Bengalees nor Oriyas, but who are mixture of both."

From various aspects, through various parameters, Yatra of Midnapore can be dissected, analyzed and categorized. If we go by a thematic study of Yatra in the context of Midnapore, we can surely observe that there are chiefly three kinds of Yatra; the ancient mythological, the largely popular folk and 'Churia,' a special form of Yatra. This categorization is based on the content and nature of the script; though there is no such bold thematic difference between the folk-story based Yatra and 'Churia' Yatra and what differentiates them is the mode of structuring and presentation.

For a long time, Yatra in Midnapore has structured itself taking subject matters from the mythological tales of ancient *Puranas*, the *Ramayana* and the *Mahabharata*. One of the most popular among these is the well-known 'Sita-Churi' (Stealing of Sita) that presents the incident of the stealing of Sita by the wicked Ravana in the *Ramayana*. As the full story delineates the honesty and prowess of lord Rama, it is known therefore as 'Ramyatra' as well. Yatra often uses some coarse devices to generate laughter or to poke some baser fun which we can unmistakably see in the primitive Italian 'Commedia dell'arte' form. Similarly, in 'Sita-Churi' or 'Ramyatra,' we witness several devices to produce laughter such as the difference between the life led by an ascetic person and a person deeply involved in worldly affairs, women's fondness of garments and dress-materials, rude and often cruel treatment of the religious persons affiliated to famous religious institutes etc. It may be mentioned here that most of these devices are used to satirize some established social and religious practices. Like the Italian 'Commedia dell'arte,' the Yatra form makes ample use of the 'masque.' Apart from the 'masque' form, it also uses a lot the dramatic device 'mask.' Monsters, demons, mythological hybrid creatures, representation of Hanuman, the golden deer in the *Ramayana* are presented through colourful masks. As A. Lal says, "Often, actors wearing masks represent well-known characters of the *Ramayana*" (451). In recent times, masking and unmasking of the characters are presented metaphorically to represent the chameleon-like nature of human beings, their tricks, hypocrisies and desperate attempt to be 'politically correct.' Another aspect of this use of mask is to poke fun in the realm of the performance.

Presentation of 'Masque' in 'Churia' Yatra

Yatra based on the folk beliefs, traditions and tales are highly popular in Midnapore. These are the Yatras which give the inhabitants of Midnapore a feeling to be connected with their cultural roots. About this folk form, D. Mukhopadhyay remarks: "It had held sway over the entire rural population for over four to six centuries." Among these folk Yatras, the most popular is the 'Yugi' Yatra. 'Yugi' is the name of a nomadic group. This group, many years ago, lived in the south-western part of Midnapore. 'Yugis' used to live outside the boundaries of traditional villages; they lived in a cluster all the time. Though they were found to be associated with the profession of cloth-weaver later on, they made their both ends meet by beggary. In 'Yugi' Yatra, players belonging to the 'Yugi' community perform prime, protagonistic roles. Often, we see the representation of how 'Yugi' clan used to do beggary with loud songs, rhymes and dance. Hence, song and dance play crucial roles in this form. The fact that is worth-mentioning at this juncture is that the term 'Yugi' incorporates a different connotation as well. It is believed that 'Yugi' is a deconstructed dialectic form of 'yogi' or 'Mahayogi'or 'Aadiyogi,' Lord Shiva; and, therefore most of the 'Yugi' performances are found to be based on stories that revolve round Lord Shiva.

'Cross-Dressing'

Though 'Yugi' Yatra gives room to 'Yugi' people as central characters, it follows a folklore known as 'Sahara Sundari.' This folklore revolves around Sahara Sundari and speaks of the struggle to possess her. Sahara Sundari is the newly married wife of a prince, a paragon of beauty, with gorgeous locks twelve feet long. While she was bathing with all her mates in a river, she lost one hair from her celebrated locks. This is found by another prince who, attracted by the beauty of her hair and imagining how beautiful then she would be, puts her in captivity. Sahara Sundari is ultimately rescued by the prince in the disguise of a

'Yugi.' In one way or other, 'Yugis' are represented with prominent force and details. Besides the thematic appropriation of mythological tales and folklore, what makes 'Yugi' Yatra interesting is the employment of 'cross-dressing.'

The third category of Yatra explored in Midnapore is 'Churia' Yatra. This form of Yatra basically unfolds the multicoloured stories of the life of Lord Krishna. In several parts of Midnapore, there are many cultural forms containing the tales of the life of Lord Krishna. In several singing and dance forms of Midnapore like Tusu and Vadu, we can see such thematic presentations. The life of Lord Krishna is full of tales and 'Churia' Yatra concentrates on that. This form is comparably shorter and takes only one or two incidents from an episode. What makes this form interesting and different from other forms is that one performance ends with the ingredients of beginning of the next one and subsequently we see interconnectivity between the 'Churia' performances. One may also say that as all 'Churia' performances follow the same source and thematic projection, hence, interconnectivity is there in all the performances. 'Krishnaleela,' 'Rasleela,' stealing of butter by Krishna, mischievous deeds of Krishna with Radha and her peers are some popular presentations of this form. 'Churia' Yatra of Midnapore has a close connection with the Oriya 'Sangitaka,' a performative form manifested mostly by dance. As 'Sangitaka' follows tales of the Krishna legends, Vrindavan and Mathura episodes, it falls in great connection with this 'Churia' Yatra form of Midnapore.

In terms of the central theme, 'Churia' Yatra and mythology-based Yatra seem similar, but the two forms have certain differences especially in terms of the mode of presentation and structure. 'Churia' performance is based on the projection of dance and songs largely; it is linear and flat. Also, it does not concentrate on any social issue; neither does it seek to address or comment on the social matters. The mythological one, on the other hand, is closely associated with society, social norms, codes and customs. Mythological form of Yatra has explored and validated itself through social messages.

Another special kind of Yatra seen in Midnapore is 'Sasthi Mangal.' Sasthi is the name of a Goddess worshipped basically by brides and mothers of the household desiring betterment of the family and children. In 'Sasthi Mangal' Yatra, the brides, by their faithful worshipping, please mother goddess Sasthi and achieve all domestic fulfilment desired by them. This form is highly ritualistic in nature. What is far more interesting to note is that in most of the cases performances have been organized in domestic premises and with active participation and contribution of the family members. Such things are done for the betterment of the household in all aspects having the blessings of mother Goddess Sasthi. This form is mostly seen in Pataspur, Belda, Sabang, Khejuri, Dantan, Mohanpur, Contai of East and West Midnapore, West Bengal.

One of the very popular and ancient Yatra forms found in Bengal in general and Midnapore in particular is 'Leto.' The term 'Leto' is perhaps a transformed colloquial form that originated from the word 'Nutu,' used in the *Rig Veda*. In several parts of Midnapore, 'leto' is a popular 'Yatra' form. In ancient times, it was performed mostly by the Muslim religious people, but later it included the Hindus to a considerable extent. Mainly lower caste Hindus involved themselves passively in the performance, and then gradually this religious difference had dispersed. 'Leto' Yatra in Midnapore is thus a symbol of communal harmony.

'Leto' performance is one of the most long-spanned performances of Midnapore. The performance takes almost whole night and that's why it has been divided into several parts known as 'Chak.' Each 'Chak' is planned and constructed by projecting a group of actors involved exclusively in that. Song is the soul of

'Leto' and most songs are found in written form. Now-a-days, famous songs of popular movies are often sung in 'Leto.'

There is hardly any documented version of Yatra in Midnapore. It is because of the fact that Yatra didn't have any written or scriptural form. There were only some expert persons who were the centre of Yatra performances and it is through their memory that Yatra has traversed a long way in Midnapore. Over and above these experts were some supreme experts; experts used to visit these supreme men and spend long hours, sometimes days, to watch the practice sessions run under the guidance of these supreme experts to imbibe the thematic and technical specificities of Yatra. The expert used to hold these specificities in his memory and apply it afterwards. Creative experts used to put their own creativity in those. In most of the cases these creative interpolations often used to come from social ends to make the performances socially didactic and relevant. Later on, the expertise of the experts began to be judged by this interpolation and application of the social dimensions with the mythological and folk tales. Among these experts, the names of Iswar Ojha and Shashanka Das are significant.

Music is one of the key elements of the Yatra. Hence, music of a Yatra performance is structured for a long time paying attention to compliment the content of the story by the projection of tune. With much attention, the tunes and lyrics of the songs are formed. Often the music, played during Yatra performance becomes loud and high-pitched. Musicians are present on both sides of the stage, carrying dholak, harmonium, tabla, flute, cymbals, trumpets etc., all used to heighten the overall dramatic effect of performances. In most of the cases, singing is done by the actors themselves which creates a 'non-illusionistic' stance.

Theatre has been 'a powerful aesthetic tool of resistance' for a long time, and Yatra, being an integral part of the folk theatre, attains prominence in this regard. Midnapore is a great name in the historical and political scenario of India as it has registered its name boldly in the freedom movement, and Yatra has contributed to this nationalistic and patriotic discourse of Midnapore to a considerable degree. During the colonial period and even in the postcolonial era, various Yatra performances, regarding the celebration of patriotism, have been organized here in Midnapore. 'Shahid Khudiram,' vindicating the sacrifice of the great patriot and youth-icon Khudiram, 'Firingee,' depicting the hegemonic oppression of the British colonial force, are among the best examples of this.

Yatra in Midnapore has a deep-rooted connection with the process of 'patronization.' Zamindars, landlords, well-known Bramhins, economically sound families used to patronize Yatras in Midnapore from the days of its origin. Apart from the economic patronization, there were esteemed social reformers and educated persons like Ram Khura and Kanai Master who used to motivate persons for Yatra production as well.

Several socio-political and cultural factors are involved in the production and enactment of a Yatra. Now-a-days, due to a healthy development of communication between Midnapore and Kolkata, 'Citpuri' tradition of Yatra in Kolkata has started to influence the Yatra form of Midnapore to much extent. Urban touches are also palpably seen now in Yatra. Not only that, it has started to incorporate urbanized operas in the performance. An alarming thing is that present-day Yatra is imbibing various 'popular' elements, often coarse and vulgar, from the commercial movies. It is gradually becoming a threat to the indigenous nature of Yatra though Yatra has introduced itself as an 'inclusive cultural and performative space.'

Nishikanta Chattopadhyay writes that in earlier time, singers and dancers forming bands, wearing colourful garments and enacting caricatures used to roam in the rural areas during any social, cultural or religious festival in order to entertain the common rural mass. This is how, perhaps, Yatra the art form was born and took an impetus later on. It is true also in the case of the birth and development of Yatra in Midnapore. Balwant Gargi remarks: "Folk art crosses the border of class, religion and country. The classical often imposes these barriers because of its esoteric nature."

Being an integral part of folk art and culture of India in general and Bengal in particular, Yatra in Midnapore started its journey from a point of being 'esoteric,' and it has moved beyond the border of class, community and religion gradually to reach the universal space.

Note: The images attached to the paper were shot by Mr. Mrinal Kanti Mahato, a teacher, a freelance researcher, an activist and a short-film maker.

Works Cited

Bayley, H.V. *Memoranda of Midnapore*, Kolkata: Bengal Secretariat Press, 1902.

Chattopadhyay, Nishikanta. *The Yatras or the Popular Dramas of Bengal,* London: Trubner, 1882.

Gargi, Balwant. *Folk Theatre of India*, USA: University of Washington Press, 1966.

Lal, Ananda. *The Oxford Companion to Indian Theatre*, New Delhi: Oxford University Press, 2008.

Mukhopadhyay, D. *Folk Art and Social Communication*, New Delhi: Ministry of Information and Broadcasting (Publication Division), Govt. of India, 1994.

Indian and Arabic Folktales: An Overview

J.R. MEGHANA
Directorate of Distance Education, Kuvempu University

Folk literature is one aspect of folklore. It is transmitted by word of mouth and it may be either or both in prose narrative and verse form. Folk literature includes myths, legends, folktales, folk epics, rituals, proverbs, riddles passed down orally through generations. Folk literature is not attributed to specific authors. Folk literature compared with written literature has many distinct features of its own. It expresses feelings, dreams and experiences which emerge from the unconscious mind of the community. It is ingrained in tradition and is preserved in memory. Therefore, oral literature is ever fresh and always on the move like a river. All literature, oral or written, springs from life, but oral literature is a projection of the innermost recesses of the social and cultural life of a society, its traditions, customs, habits, behaviour, rites, etc.

Folk literature is found everywhere in a variety of expressions and it may differ from place to place. Major forms of folk literature such as folk songs imply the use of the musical tradition that varies greatly from one area to another. A folk song can be described as traditional music of unknown authorship, which is transmitted by the medium of orality, Indian folk music is diverse because of India's vast cultural diversity. Fables are another form of folk literature, such as the famous Aesop's fables with animals acting according to their real nature. A number of tales like these are told by storytellers in many parts of the world with appropriate morals and values. Similarly, every culture has a collection of wise sayings known as proverbs which offer guidelines to live life properly. On the other hand, a riddle is a type of verbal expression in which something is kept concealed the answer of which is demanded through guess work. The folk tale is a story handed down verbally from one generation to another. Each storyteller added something new to the existing stories, making them more interesting and fascinating as the ages passed. The folk tales bear the characteristics of culture and customs of the society from which they have originated. Folk tales are not mere stories. They contain the standards of what is good and what is wrong. They represent the shared views of the moral statements of the community.

In folklore the narrator or the folk singer carries on a tradition learned from other narrators and the narrative is delivered to a living audience. It may be said that the listeners have heard this material many times before and that it has a vigorous life in the community, and if acceptable to the listeners, the story or song or proverb or riddle will be repeated over and over again as long as they appeals to men and women through the ages and over long geographic distances. Interestingly, children are allured and overwhelmed by folk tales. Their popularity springs from imaginative characters, supernatural elements. They possess an appeal to the unconscious assimilation of these values by means of narration and role play. Therefore, folk tales are recognized as a source of learning for children. Historically, the development of storytelling goes back to the times when societies were being formed. For millennia, stories have moulded children's character by carrying many social, moral and cultural values in the form of literature. It is crucial for children to learn about their own cultural heritage and the cultures of others because developing positive attitudes toward our culture and the cultures of others is necessary for both social and personal development. Folk tales have been an eternal part of every culture since ages. A folk tale is a traditional story which is originally passed on orally by the people living in a community. When it comes to folk tales in India, the country of diverse religions, languages and cultures, they have a complete range of tales. All these ancient stories have been passed down from one generation to the other generation, creating a bond of traditional values with the present-day generation.

India is the home many world famous folk epics, the *Ramayana* and the *Mahabharata. Panchatantra*, *Jataka Tales* and *Hitopadesha* have been in existence for a long time. Scholars, saints, and writers have kept the oral traditions and folk tales alive by writing down many a tale. *Panchatantra* is a collection of fables, originally composed in the 2nd century B.C. but dating is still more difficult. The purpose behind its composition was to implant moral values and governing skills in the young sons of the King. These stories communicate the essence of diplomacy, relationships, politics and administration. *Jataka Tales* are supposed to have been composed between 300 B.C. and 500 A.D. to disseminate knowledge and morality to mankind. Originally written in Pali language, *Jataka Tales* have been translated into different languages around the world. The luminous fables of *Jataka Tales* are intended to impart values of self-sacrifice, morality and honesty. Written in a witty, lucid, attractive style, and a well-structured language, these stories not only give children an immense pleasure of reading but also enrich their minds with moral and social values. These tales contribute towards shaping a strong moral mindset of young children.

India has many such memorable stories collections, such as *Akbar Birbal, Tenali Rama, Vikram Betal, Singhasan Battisi* which serve the noble and genuine purpose by imparting information about their culture along with instilling moral understanding in the reader. *Akbar Birbal* is a collection of stories of the Mughal King Akbar and one of his famous courtiers Birbal who was very witty and had great presence of mind. He was so quick and prompt in his reply to any question of the King that the King was always left speechless. With time, Birbal became his most trusted courtier and advisor. Thus the stories inform the readers about the life of people in Akbar's kingdom and also give a sense of moral understanding and accurate perception to follow the right path in any adverse circumstances.

Tenali Rama is a collection of stories about Krishnadevaraya Raya, the ruler of Vijayanagar, and one of his courtiers Tenali Rama. Tenali Rama was a very clever and witty person. Like the stories of *Akbar and Birbal,* the stories of *Tenali Rama* have also become a part of our folklore. These stories are so popular that people of all ages like them and with time, their popularity has increased. These stories have enduring qualities. The character of Tenali Rama not only entertains the reader with his witty repartee and dexterity but also enlightens the reader with his wisdom and honesty and also reflects the moral behaviour which should be conducted for the upliftment of humankind. The life of the people of Vijayanagar of that time is also reflected in these stories. Thus these stories also have a historical value.

Vikram and Betal Stories or *Betal Pachisi* written nearly 2,500 years ago contains spellbinding stories told to the wise King Vikramaditya by the wily ghost Betal. Each story ends with a riddle and the King Vikramaditya being the wisest, the most noble and virtuous man with excellent skills, has to give a moral to each story which was narrated to him by the ghost Betal. Another collection of Indian folk tales is *Singhasan Battisi*. The title literally means thirty-two tales of the throne. The thirty-two tales tell about the deeds and adventures of King Vikramaditya and his bravery, virtues, wit and wisdom. *Here Comes Holi: The Festival of Colours* is the story of a young prince Prahlad and king Hirnakasypu. The story brings out the fun and festivity of Holi with its mythical significance. India remains one of the world's richest sources of folk tales. Folk literature is not merely a carrier of culture or philosophical vision, but rather an expression of self-reflections, deep insight, simple life, and the path of righteousness contained in traditions.

Similar to India, the Arabic world abounds with legends, folk tales and myths which reflect the cultural history, social customs, morals, values and religious beliefs. The Arabic folk tales are a source of entertainment, moral lessons and a commentary on religious customs, similar to Indian folk tales. These compositions are rich in detail, clear in delivery, smooth in translation, presented with apparent ease. These folk tales have a richly descriptive background and information on the Arab world. The Arabic folk tales bring together stories from a variety of Arab countries and social groups within these countries. They carefully reflect the notion of honour which pervades the Arab tribal society. This complex system of values is often romanticized by the Arabs and revered as the quintessence of their civilization.

The Arabic tales embody many characteristics. They reflect the social values the Arabs have in common and discuss the position and roles of men and women in society. Faith in God is usually expressed through the hero, who uses his belief to achieve the main task. An all-powerful King is also depicted and the presence of the supernatural elements is a very important component of most Arabic tales and legends. Since the tribal structure was the nucleus of social and political life for a very long period in Arabic history, the values of such a culture influenced the folktales and legends. Very often, hospitality and kindness to guests and strangers is essential for survival in the desert. Attributes such as courage, honesty, honour, hospitality, generosity, and loyalty are emphasized. The hero is defined by characteristics such as self-respect, bravery in war, protecting the weak, and helping the poor.

An Arab's faith in God is strongly reflected in folktales passed down through the generations. In a large number of these tales, the hero is said to act according to God's will. For instance, a poor man accepts his poverty because it is his destiny decided by God. God may answer the wishes of good people, such as, granting a child or bestowing wealth. In addition, God also punishes the evil characters that cause trouble for the protagonists.

It is interesting to note that although folk tales might include supernatural and magical elements, they are usually based on real life events that stem from the Arab culture. Social values like courage and honesty are often preserved in the legends and folk tales. Imagination and creativity in these tales add to their beauty and entertaining capacity without minimizing the influence of real life events. The Arabic folk tales display the social structures of the community and values of the Arabian community. The prominent feature of the Arabian folk tales is the position and roles of men and women in the Arab society. The faith in the presence of the Almighty is usually expressed through the male protagonist, who deploys his belief in the power of the Almighty and his own determination and skill to meet the challenges which come to the protagonist of the story to complete the mission. In these tales, the powerful kings or heroes are also depicted. The presence of the supernatural beings and supernatural elements is a significant component of most Arabic folk tales.

Most of the tales have a significant moral that teaches the reader the ethical values, basically the attribute to discriminate between the right and the wrong. One of the most common morals in these Arabian folk tales is tolerance which leads to success, satisfaction and adequate contentment which keep one out of menacing troubles and loyalty and loyal behaviour which is always rewarded. A thief particularly will be caught and discovered and later punished by the authorities. All these lessons through the medium of the Arabic folk tales are meant to enhance the set of values that include Arab culture and make it unique and interesting to read and delve deep into the tales which arouse curiosity in the conscience and psyche of the reader and also educate them. The very famous Arabic folk tale collection is *The Arabian Nights.*

Arabic folk tales circulated orally for thousands of years are rooted in ancient and medieval culture and folklore with Egyptian, Persian, and Mesopotamian influences. When Arabic folk tales were first written down formally in the 14th century, they were in the Syrian Arabic manuscript. Some of the most famous Arabic folk tales are contained in *One Thousand and One Nights*, compiled during the Islamic Golden Age. The origins of the stories in this collection are complex. Iraqi influence is added to the stories, and the original few stories can be traced back to India and Persia in the 8th century. They are a rare gem for the literary world.

The Arabian Nights is a collection of tales from the Islamic Golden Age, compiled by various authors over hundreds of years. Though each collection features different stories, they are all centred around the frame story of the Sultan Shaharyar and his wife, Scheherazade.

Hatim Stories is a book about the adventures of Hatimtai, the king of Yemen. Though these stories were written long back, they remain popular even today. The qualities that inspire and fascinate people are kindness, generosity, etc. which are displayed by the hero of the story.

The tales themselves are filled with magic, charm, and romance which mark folk tales around the world. Young people fall in love at the first sight, clever men amass fortunes, mothers protect their young ones, wicked people are outsmarted, and the wise and religious are rewarded. The tales are filled with villains who capture the readers' imagination and are thwarted only by the clever, the witty and the brave. Animal tales, humorous tales, and foolish tales, all have their place in the timeless Arabian folk tale collections. Children will be captivated by the stories and demand that they read and reread which should only delight the reader and enhance their cognitive perception as the stories are full of wit and wisdom and also give an insight in the rich tradition and cultural heritage of the particular country.

The folk tales also serve as an effective tool of entertainment along with educating the readers in instilling the moral and ethical code of conduct in the psyche of the readers and are enjoyed by all age groups. The hidden morals inside each tale, and the concocted ideas, make the folktales not only restricted to the children but also to adults and the old alike. So far, a comparative study between the Indian and the Arabic classic literature has not been conducted. They have been studied in isolation rather than in reference to each other.

Bibliography

Akbar Birbal Tales. Noida: Tiny Tot Publications, 2016.

A.R., Saleh. *Arab Folklore.* UNESCO. Folk Media and Mass Media in Population Communication, Paris. France. UNESCO: 1977.

Burton, F. Richard Sir. *1001 Arabian Nights.* Jaico, 2014.

Chittenden, Varick. Exhibit Curator. From the Brochure of the Folk Arts Exhibition, Out of the Ordinary produced by Gallery Association of New York State: 1995.

Dua, Shyam. *Jataka Tales.* Noida: Tiny Tot Publications, 2015.

Genres: An Introduction. Logan, UT: Utah State University Press: 1986.

Hatim Stories. Noida: Tiny Tot Publications, 2014.

Munshi, Mohammad Ghulam. *Baital Pachisi.* Bombay: Oriental Press. 1868.

Pandya, Atul Meenal, *Here Comes Holi: The Festival of Colours.* Chennai: Meera Publications, 2003.

Ryder, W. Arthur. *Panchatantra.* Mumbai: Jaico, 2015.

Singhasan Battisi. Mumbai: Jaico, 2016.

Tenali Rama Tales. Noida: Tiny Tot Publications. 2014.

"Veer Rasa" in the Heroic Ballad of Maharana Pratap

JAYSHREE SINGH
Bhupal Nobles' University, Udaipur

The folklore of Rajasthan, more specifically the folklore of Mewar consists of the moral, spiritual, emotional and physical sensitivities. Folklore has inspired the world with its essence; factual experience transposed into folk songs can be examined through the study of popular culture. In the Mewar region of Rajasthan, folklore, if categorized, there will be significant segmented units which illustrate the folks' lifestyle, cultural rituals/ rites, social customs and religious traditions. The folklore concerning 'Veer Rasa' represents formidable political foreground, refusal to yield, and the 'Will to Power' environment. The criteria of the prevalence of the particular, popular folklore of a place seem to be couched in the knowledge about the subject to power and a potential for self-image as superior with unconscious positivity and rationality. The present paper explores the warrior, Maharana Pratap's valour and gallantry, patriotism and nationalism through folklore.

Sometimes a certain purpose resonates in folklore on festive occasions in local traditions and customs. Folklore corresponds to the sense of social interaction and consciousness which is carried forward from one generation to another, so the thoughts of folk are elicited in varied forms in Indian culture. Hasu Yajnik (Yasu Nagnik) in his essay, "Myths and Mythology" describes that the folk narrative popularly influences mentality, culture, tradition, dialect and society of a particular geographical area. He writes:

> In this way ... something may come from the myth and something may be the creation of the popular psychology of the later period. This process is like that of a dialect, a language or a style of singing and a melody. The classical form of a language is determined only by culling together the characteristics of different dialects, and at a later stage the language becomes the element that keeps the dialect bound up. And, then the dialect gets nourished and developed by incorporating the structure of language. After the prevalence of the fixed, uniform and allied styles of singing, the tunes and their groups employed in such folk styles of singing are analyzed, and the types of tunes, their nature and their context utilization are inferred, and on the basis of them the structure of the new melody is grasped. At the later stage, melodies themselves bind up such a style of singing and generate newer and fresh folk styles of singing. (21)

The critic points out that at the elementary level, the sound and language shape the narrative, which is based on the unanimous idea regarding an individual in a society, and this subsequently is carried to a secondary level to state reflections between the cause and effect relationship, "between the dialect, the language, the style of singing, the melody, the oral tradition and the written tradition considered to be the classical one or the tradition of the folk literature and individual literature is complicated" (*Ibid.*).

Before probing more into the development of folklore devoted to Maharana Pratap, the illustrious scion of Mewar, it is apt to understand the process of imitation which is full of unpremeditated spontaneity, folksongs, especially that generate spark of inspiration, power, light, courage and determination among the folk, which generation after generation have become the living narrative sources of expression, myths, legends and ecstatic singing.

In the context it will be proper to briefly discuss the 'Rasa' theory evolved by the Indian sage Bharatmuni (1st century BC-3rd century). Based on the Ranga manch Rasa means emotions evoked in the spectators by the dramatic art shown on the stage, that is when the characters enact the dramatic action, the folksingers perform, the spectators watch or purge their sentiments (later on when the readers read or critics interpret, and the writer create literary composition) encapsulating the central element of aesthetics and transcendentalized experience. Bharatmuni's *Natyashastra* is a detailed treatise and handbook on dramatic art. It is the oldest extant work on Indian Poetics and deals with all aspects of dramaturgy of the classical Sanskrit theatre. The greatest merit of 'Rasa' (emotion evoked) theory is that it has erected its magnificent edifice on the solid foundation of the commonality of human feelings and emotions (Bhatia 10-12). According to Dimock, Indian Poetics may be appropriated for Indian literature.

This paper will focus on Mewar folklore available on Maharana Pratap, in relation to the following points:

- The warrior's valour and gallantry; patriotism and nationalism,
- The birth and saga of life which symbolically refers to sacrifice and martyrdom.
- The semiotic properties that present discourse analysis on the idea to protect the nation's sovereignty or region's integrity.
- The relevance of how the brave deeds in history are a source of inspiration for young Indians.
- An examination of how their loyalty interfaces with nation's totality in the present situation of the country.

Maharana Pratap, the glorious scion of Mewar, is remembered for his being invincible to the Mughal Emperor Akbar. He remained dauntless in face of his enemies' invasion on Mewar because of his unbreakable spirit of freedom. Maharana Pratap was the torchbearer for the Indian rulers. His inherent drive of being a ruler of sovereign state left an indelible mark on the other provincial dynasties to carry out freedom struggle for the integration of society and their ruling states. His inspiration for integration and independence set an example for other kings of Indian subcontinent, who surrendered their sovereignty due to the fear of being diminished and destroyed. Maharana Pratap's valour, perseverance and fearless spirit made him persistently stand against subjugation. He not only inspired people of Rajputana but showed the path to the future generations of India for standing until their last breath for their motherland even in the toughest conditions.

The Sikhs in Punjab, Hyder Ali and Tipu Sultan in Mysore, the Gorkhas in Nepal were inspired by the persona of Maharana Pratap. Historiography of Medieval India has failed to justify the real and multifaceted contribution of Maharana Pratap. Marxist historiography much relied on Persian sources and has failed to explore archival records available in Mewar, Punjab and Sindh. Mewar-Mughal feud was not just limited to the siege of Chittore or the Battle of Haldighati. Researchers have failed to explore the long struggle of the Mewar Kingdom after 1576 till the death of Maharana Pratap and later with Aurangzeb. Even during war time extraordinary ability of governance was displayed by Maharana Pratap. As an administrator, he was the harbinger of social justice and integration. He meticulously managed the resources of all kinds. From agriculture to trade to extraction of mining resources, all was managed with an extraordinary efficiency. The struggle of central powers with the Rajputana was one of the glorious chapters of the medieval history of India.

This paper analyses the poetic portions of Rajasthani folk literature, that have elevated the dialect and culture of the Rajasthani language in order to transmit the significance, magnificence and ardent fervour of the noble warrior king of Mewar region. The poetic song entitled "Akbar and Maharana Pratap" (the lyric's metric style is in Sannaur linguistic pattern of regional Mewari dialect) has been derived from *Pracheen Rajasthani Geet—Part 3* edited by the poet Mohan Singh. Here, the poet sings praises for Maharana Pratap's war diplomacy, strategy and operations performed against Akbar, the Mughal Emperor of his times, who attempted thrice to establish his reign and supremacy over the tribal area of Mewar. The writer conveys that Maharana

Pratap daringly staked his life and was always on his feet, well-equipped with arms and armour. He thus became a bottleneck for Akbar's dream of the expansion of his empire in the Southern part of Rajasthan. Akbar had never come across such a true, noble and brave-heart warrior of blue blood. All other kings feared him and surrendered. The following lines of the song reflect this feeling:

> Dhar Vihar Pratap Khadag Dhar, Suj Bisar Nah Pakkar Saer!
> Akbar Uber Maal Aadhado, Oeeyeney Sevag Bhup Aaner!!
>
> (*Pracheen Rajasthani Geet* Part VI, 32)

Another song entitled "The inability of poets to raise praise for Maharana Pratap's valour in the battlefield" is also a lyric in Dingal verse with pattern of short stressed syllables and voiced plosive consonant sounds:

> Badhiyo Vasaav Taney Badd Pattan, Rana Ajuwaalta Rahi!
> Ekani Kaleh Jitey Gun Aankha, karey Jitobijoy Kaleh!!
> Aey Brasaav Vadhey Udawat, Matey n Nis Basur Til Maat!
> Paar n Paatal Tanna Pravaad Paar n Gunn Kehta Kavipaat!!
>
> (*Pracheen Rajasthani G*eet Part III, 51)

The lines convey that before the poets in admiration for grandiose of Maharana Pratap could prepare themselves with the maturity and ripeness to sing song in praise of chivalry and gallantry, another war started between the Mewar state and the centrally located powerful Akbar, the emperor of Hindustan. Maharana Pratap with his power-driven, invincible, dauntless spirit advanced to save independence and dignity of the Mewar Kingdom soon after the battles of Deewer and Haldighati against Akbar in 1576, but the poets could not get appropriate words to weave garland of appreciation in the glory of the noble warrior.

Most of the earlier lyrics were composed in Pingal language, which was considered an ancient formation of verbal poetic culture and form of Prakrit, popular language in Rajasthan and nearby areas, which gave birth to an opposite lyrical pattern namely Dingal, which was primarily a language of warlike intonations, while Pingal was a language of love and softspokenness. There have been many Rajasthani poets and writers who had written in Dingal. It is a language of high tone and requires a specific style of speaking. It was primarily used by *Charans* (a class of bards that used to accompany warriors to the warfront) to motivate them by praising their martial exploits. Several Rajput kings have also written poems in Dingal, particularly Maharaja Man Singh Rathore of Marwar who reigned from 1803 to 1843. Actually, Dingal is neither a language nor a dialect. It is a mode of rendering poetry, with a distinct flair of its own, an ode that has sprouted from the original Rajasthani language. The pre- and the post-Haldighati battle poets have used 'the interpolations and insertion of text' with allusions from Hellenic, Persian and indigenous vocabulary and symbols. Such usage of diction and metre indicate the historical context during compilation of works (Patrick 264-65). The Pingala style of lyrical pattern and metre (which is also ascribed to Devanagari style of metrical pattern) is used in the Rajasthani poetic manuscripts entitled *Pingala Sutras* or *Chand Sutra*, one of the oldest Hindu Treatise on Sanskrit prosody (2nd or 6th century BC) to have survived into the modern era (Pingle 238-41). The compositions in Pingala metrical tradition signify large and significant changes in metre; the metrical template of Pingala style do follow versification tradition of Sanskrit metres, yet the structure of words in linguistic material sense signify temporality (line strength and constraints of metre appear often unlimited in number) and a periodicity (a metrical pattern constitute arbitrary syllable sequences without any noticeable periodic repetition)—i.e. there emerges the complex mappings of linguistic material to these poetic templates that sing the praise of valour Maharana Pratap's valour (Deo 47-63).

Most of the figurative poetic verses sung by tribes and native folks in the Rajasthani metrical pattern called Pingal present Rajasthani poets' ability of being polyglots i.e. using Sanskrit, Persian and Latin sounds in their compositions, although they have retained indigeneity of the Mewari semantic, syntactic and lexical structure in their usage of words. Pingal style of poetic metre lent to the composition a comparative toughness in context of the revelation of 'Veer rasa,' i.e. a persona exuding a sense of fearlessness against deceit and injustice through one's emotions and gestures, will, thought, action and response. According to Motilal Banarsidas, Pingala used to be an example of a medieval Sanskrit prosody of poetic metres for the reason that it has 'polymorphic linear sequence' in the metrical composition which was to elaborate a special level of reverence for their contemporary ruling kings. It was also to attribute the godly perfection and beauty of metres to the incarnations of divine origin as their chieftains and kings. Since the character of ruling kings was praised as being equal to Gods, so the folk songs idealized the legendary figures which may be called, to use Carlyle's words, 'hero-worship.'

One of the famous poets of heroic writing in Mewar region of Rajasthani metrical tradition is Thakur Nathu Singh Mahiyariya, born in a *charan* family in the princely state of Mewar. He wrote many books such as *Veer Satsai*, *Hadi Rani Shatak* etc. He pays his tribute to the great and glorious king of Mewar in these words:

> Puran Pavitra Partap, Haey Charitra Tero! Padhivey Tey Maet Dett Sankat Tritap Key!!
> Mere Janivey Mey Ram Nam Sau Mahan Mantra! Path Key Karey Tey Hathi Jaat Punj Paap Key!!
> Chhatrin Ko Maan Abhmaan Jaati Hindun Ko! Jaapey Phal Dehey Sam Sanjeevan Jaap Key!
> Aaap hi Ki Vastu Taantey Aap Adhikari Yaakey! Rann Shri Pratap Nath Samarprit Aap Key!! (45-46)

The poet's heart is overwhelmed with the fearless bravery of warrior-king Maharana Pratap, whose undaunted brave leadership inspired many rulers of princely states to take refuge in his saviour-shield against oppressive forces and many dared to stand against humiliation and attack on their sovereignty. The writer regrets that there were no poets during the imperial times of the glorious Hindu scion Maharana Pratap, who could compose and sing the glories of the war-hero.

Nathu Singh Mahiyariya in his book *Jhalamaan* (2016) writes about the popularly known immemorial feats of Maharana Pratap and expresses his passionate praise for the King of Mewar:

> Haldghat Rann Ditithiya, Ik Saathey Treya Bhaan!
> Rann Udai Ravi Astga, Madhya Tapt Makwaan!! (90-91)

He says that it was an exceptional coincidence that in the battle-field of Haldighat (18 June 1576), three suns shone at the same time. The first was the illustrious saviour of Hindu religion Maharana Pratap; the second was the bright sun that rises every-day in the morning and moves through the sky towards the western mountains to set during evening hours; the third sun was Jhalamaan; on that day on battlefield, the scorching midday Sun plunged ahead to stand by the side of brave warrior Maharana Pratap. The composition is in Dingal metrical pattern, which depicts self-propelling sounds and tones to raise sense of honour, pride, dignity and self-respect in the freedom-fighting spirit of warriors, soldiers, kings and nobles. This metrical style emanates elements of temporality while struggling against atrocious hostile invader on the battlefield.

A nineteenth century poet, Kaviraj Shyamaldas wrote *Veer Vinod* (Heroes' Delight), an authentic compilation of the history of Mewar. The poet Yogidas and Raghunath Rupak have talked of 72 kinds of Rajasthani songs, among which is one of the famous 'small sannaur.' It consists of charans, each charan consisting of 16 or 15 syllables which ends with the /s/ sound. One such song is entitled 'Snake-Charmer Akbar failed to subjugate the Sheshnag Maharana Pratap':

> Aalape Jaiye Garudh Akbari, Deepey Treesa-Sat-kul-Daw!
> Rann Ses Vasudha Khatra Rakhann, Ragin a Pantriyo Aahirau
> Manidhar Chatradhar Aawar Duley Mann, Taidhar Rajdhar Seedh Tann!
> Pungidhar Patsaah Phirtey, Phirey Kamal Tan Sahas Phann

Ghadh Gadh Raaf Raaf Dhakhey Gah, Renn Vans Krit Laaj Ares!
Pandar Vaes Naad Aann Peenag Saes Na Aayo Paat Nares
Aani Aaya Uspati Aawaheen, Bhuaway Bhuawang Huey Dal Bhang!
Rahiyo Renn Khatri Dhram Rana, Saet Urang Kalodhar Sang
(*Pracheen Rajasthani Geet*, Part III, 41-42)

These lines glorify the legendary warrior Maharana Pratap, who as an incarnation of the Supreme Creator Lord Vishnu of Hindus, with all his might smashed all barriers, atrocities, manoeuvres of the demon invader Akbar. These poetic verses also signify the travestied form of Dingal language, indicating linguistic alterations derived from host traditions and foreign instantiations owing to multicultural integration and multilingual pattern of Indian subcontinent during the medieval times. At surface level, the amalgamation of vernaculars such as Marathi, Pali and religious influences of Hinduism and Buddhism are felt.

Most of the Rajasthani verses composed on Maharana Pratap praise him for his leadership qualities, his triumphs in breaking the morale of his enemies, his victories in bloodsheds caused by the oppressive forces to subdue him at any cost. The following couplet from 'Virudhchchatthari,' written by Dursa Hadda in 76 couplets, and included in *Pracheen Rajasthani Geet Part I*, edited by the poet Govardhan Sharma, expresses heroism and sacrifice of the Shining Star of Mewar. The poet says:

Akbar Kila Aanek, Fateh Kiya Nij Phaujasu!
Akkal Chaley na Ek, Paddhar Ladey Pratapsi!!
Akbar Tal Aaram, Pekhey Jahar Pratapsi!
Akbar Meygath Achh, Manjhal Dhatt Dhumey Masat!!
Panchanan Path Bhachch, Patakey Chhada Pratapsi!
Ghat Su Oghat Ghat, Ghasiyo Akbariye Ghano!! (Saraswat 53-54)

Dursa Hadda, a warrior and self-respecting nobleman, was one of the famous poets. Although he was part of Akbar's forces, yet he untiringly appreciated the legendary gallant Maharana Pratap. He further wrote:

Sukh Hit Khayal Samaaj, Hindu Akbar Bas Hua!

Rasilo Mrigraj Paje n Raan Pratap si!! (Bhati 201)

He says that Akbar too could not resist showing his strength and intelligence so as to meet Maharana Pratap face to face.

Kanyhialal Sethi's famous lyrics in *Pathal Aur Pithal* represent Dingal poetic culture. It is a reflection of heteroglossia i.e. poetic verses consisting of the co-existence of distinct varieties within a single language. Dingal diction and versification of Rajasthani verses show inclusion of polymorphic linear sequences or the linguistic material consisting of such structure of sounds and syllables in words that seem often unlimited in number with regard to following constraints of metre. There is admixture of Sanskrit, Pali, Prakrit, Marathi, Punjabi and Rajasthani. There are arbitrary voiced sounds of consonants coined with syllable sequences without any noticeable periodic repetition.

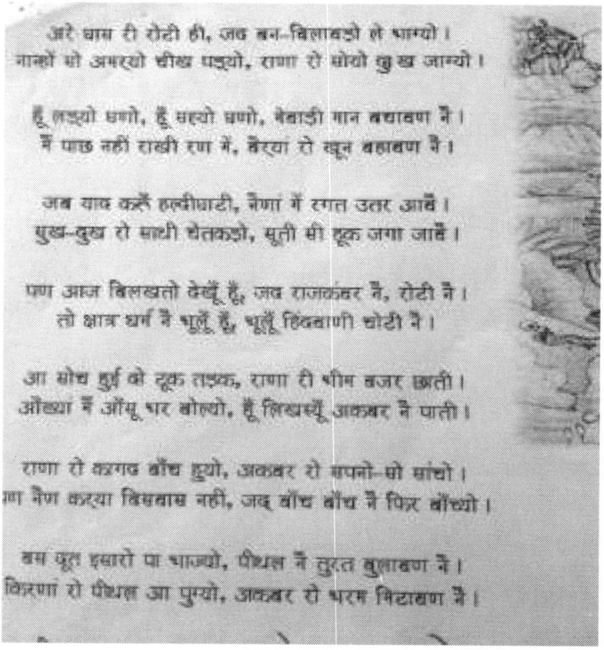
अरे घास री रोटी ही, जद बन-बिलावड़ो ले भाग्यो।
नान्हों सो अमर्‌यो चीख पड्यो, राणा रो सोयो दुख जाग्यो।

हूँ लड्यो घणो, हूँ सह्यो घणो, मेवाड़ी मान बचावण नै।
मैं पाछ नहीं राखी रण में, बैर्‌यां रो खून बहावण नै।

जद याद करूँ हल्दीघाटी, नैणां में रगत उतर आवै।
सुख-दुख रो साथी चेतकड़ो, सूती सी हूक जगा जावै।

पण आज बिलखतो देखूँ हूँ, जद राजकंवर नै, रोटी नै।
तो क्षात्र धर्म नै भूलूँ हूँ, भूलूँ हिंदवाणी चोटी नै।

आ सोच हुई दो टूक तड़क, राणा री भीम बजर छाती।
आँख्यां में आँसू भर बोल्यो, हूँ लिखस्यूँ अकबर नै पाती।

राणा रो कागद बाँच हुयो, अकबर रो सपनो-सो सांचो।
ण नैण कर्‌या बिसवास नहीं, जद बाँच बाँच नै फिर बाँच्यो।

बस दूत इसारो पा भाज्यो, पीथल नै तुरत बुलावण नै।
किरणां रो पीथल आ पूग्यो, अकबर रो भरम मिटावण नै।

Pathal Aur Pithal narrates how one day when Rana's family had nothing else to eat, his son Amar was given a bread made from grass seeds. But even that piece of bread was snatched by a wild cat in the jungle. Akbar could not believe his eyes, and sent for the poet Pathal, who was a great admirer of Rana's resolve and valour. Pithal was shattered to see this critical state of Rana and his family and wrote to Rana few lines that shook Maharana Pratap back into his original resolve to keep fighting against Akbar. Here Pathal also means Partha (Arjun) that was another name for Maharana Pratap.

In his famous epic poem *Haldighati*, Shyam Narayan Pandey sings the glory of the greatest warrior of Rajasthan:

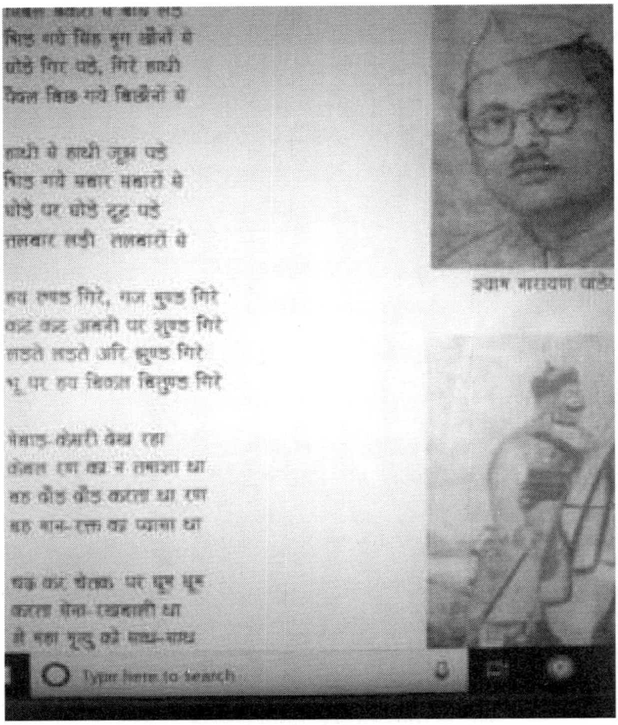

To conclude, it may be said that almost all the lyrical works and compositions concerning the greatest persona Maharana Pratap of the Southern Rajasthan region, and all songs and ballads dedicated to this celebrated warrior seek attention of historians, folklorists, linguists, and literary scholars for multiple dimensions and perspectives towards keeping the patriotic fervor embodied in the heroic character who will never go out of the memory of the folk mind, creative artists and singers.

Works Cited

Baarhat, Kesari Singh. *Pratap Charitra*. Rajasthani Granthagar, Jodhpur, 2011.

Banarsidass, Motilal. *Kalattvakosa: A Lexicon of Fundamental Concepts of the Indian Arts*, 401.

Bettina, Baumer. *Chhand Sutra*, trans. Kapila Vatsayan. 1992.

Bhati, Hukum Singh, ed. *Yug Purush: Maharana Pratap*. Pratap Shodh Pratishthan, Udaipur, 1991.

Bhatia, Namita. *IOSR Journal of Humanities and Social Science*, 21: 10, Ver. 9, 2016, 10-12. iosrjournals.org.

Deo, Ashwin S. "The Metrical Organisation of Sanskrit Verse," *Journal of Linguistics*, Vol. 43, 2007.

Leitch, Vincent B. (2001). *The Norton Anthology of Theory and Criticism*. Norton, 135-54.

Mahiyariya, Nathu Singh. *Jhala Maan*. Pratap Shodh Pratishthan, Udaipur, 2016.

Mohan Singh, Kavraj, ed. *Pracheen Rajasthani Geet*, Part III. Sahitya Sansthan, Rajasthan Vishwa Vidyapeeth, Udaipur, 2014.

Patrick, Olivelle. *Collected Essays: Language, Texts and Society*. Ferenze University Press, 2008, 264-65.

Pingale, B.A. *Pingala Sutra*. 1898, 238-41.

Sarawat, Rawat. *Dursa Hadda*. Sahitya Akademi, 1993.

Sethi, Kanhaiyalal. *Pathal Aur Pithal*. Geet-Kavita.com. Blog. Rajiv Krishna Saxena. Wordpress.com.

Sharma, Govardhan, ed. *Pracheen Rajasthani Geet,* Part VI. Sahitya Sansthan, Rajasthan Vishwa Vidyapeeth, Udaipur, 2013.

Shyam Narayan Pandey, Haldighati Yudh. Geet-Kavita.com.

Solanki, Ram Singh. *O Bhai Pratap Ro*, ed. Devkaran Singh Rupaheli. Pratap Shodh Pratishthan, Udaipur, 1997.

Yagnik, Hasu. "Myths and Mythology." *Folklore of Gujarat*, trans. N.M. Kansara. New Delhi: National Book Trust, 2001. pp 21-22.

Haryanvi *Karke*: A Peek into Folk Wisdom

JAGDISH BATRA
O.P. Jindal Global University, Sonepat

While describing the tombs of the villagers resting eternally describing the tombs of the villagers resting eternally beneath "those rugged elms, that yew-tree's shade/ Where heaves the turf in many a mould'ring heap," Thomas Grey, in his celebrated poem "An Elegy Written in a Country Churchyard," refers to the "rude forefathers" and "The short and simple annals of the poor." It must be said, however, that these "short and simple annals of the poor" have a lot of rustic wisdom about them and these only need space and elaboration. The forefathers will then not appear "rude," i.e., simple and naïve village folk, but they are the torch bearers of folk wisdom that flashes a light into the corners of our minds with insight. Looking at the village community in the Haryana countryside too evokes tales of life experiences of these people which are available in scores of stories and wisecracks that characterize the rural discourse. This paper will demonstrate the Haryanvi *karke* (songs) sung in short couplets form impregnated with timeless values of folk wisdom as the spice of agrarian communities of Haryana.

Haryanvi[1] folklore is remarkable for its very rich songs that have been passed on as word of mouth from generation to generation. After the state of Haryana was carved out of composite Punjab way back in 1966, and some years after the establishment of the universities at Kurukshetra and Rohtak the academic community, particularly those teaching Hindi, took keen interest in documenting the unwritten material comprising *raganis* or songs sung by professional singers, *swaangs* or action songs performed by professional or amateur groups, songs sung by individuals, particularly women on certain occasions like marriage or child-birth, *karke* or wisecracks, puzzles for amusement, and so on. There are songs which are sung when women go to a fair, or even to fetch water from the village well, situated some distance away from home or sit on the spinning wheel; songs while they dress up and songs which are sung as lullabies to put the infants to sleep. And of course, songs are there for different festivals, gods, goddesses, etc.

Besides songs, there is a wide variety of stories or *kisse* as these are called. A large number of songs and stories have been documented by scholars like Shankar Lal Yadav, Raja Ram Shastri, Devi Shankar Prabhakar, Santram Deswal, Rajbir Deswal and Jai Bhagwan Kaushik. While most writers have written in Hindi, some like Sumer Chand have published books in chaste Haryanvi dialect. An interesting insight into the importance of such stories is given in a *kissa* documented by Sumer Chand in the Introduction to his book *Mhaari Daadi Naani wali Kahni*. It goes like this: There was a village woman who knew a story which she had not shared with anyone. The story within her felt so much frustrated that it started looking for an opportunity to escape from the body of the woman. One night, when the woman's husband was away and she was waiting for his return, she went to sleep with her mouth open. The story within now got the chance and escaped through her open mouth. While going out of the house, the story got transformed into a male sandal (*juti*) placed at the entrance.

When the woman's husband came home, he saw the male sandal at the door and got suspicious about his wife sleeping with some other man. He got dismayed and went to the village temple where he slept at the platform (*chabutara*) around the *peepal* tree. It was a custom that when the oil in the earthen lamps lighting the village houses got exhausted and the lamps got extinguished, these were brought to be placed in the temple.

That night the lamp from this man's house arrived late. When the other lamps asked this lamp the reason for delay, this lamp told them about the "story" coming out of woman's body and turning into *juti*. The man overheard the story and was convinced about his wife's fidelity and went back home. The moral of the story is that if a story is there, it ought to be told otherwise it will get one into trouble. Clearly, these stories have the pattern of the fables of *Panchatantra*, or we can say these have the postmodern element of magic realism. Such tales apart from their moral values constitute belief narratives or legends prevalent in many societies and communities. But in this paper attention is drawn to the *karke*, a popular form of folk song in Haryana.

The *karke* (plural form of *karka*) or witty sayings are as mentioned above are full of folk wisdom. As distinguished from proverbs which are in the form of a phrase or a short sentence *karke* are short verse couplets or at best a quatrain written in chaste Haryanvi dialect so as to appeal to the village folk. The term *karke* has a humorous connotation, but it is not all humour. Most such verses are looked upon as having been composed by village forefathers, who were not "rude" in the Grey-ian terms, but worldly and spiritually wise people. These *karke* concern all areas of human activity but agriculture finds focus in a big way for obvious reasons. In fact, these find an uncanny resemblance with the Greek poet Hesiod's *Works and Days* wherein the legendary poet doled out advice to his lazy brother Perses on farm management, animal husbandry and social relationships.

In an agricultural state like Haryana, the vocation of a farmer is supposed to be the highest, followed by trade, employment and begging in that order: *Uttam Khet madham byopar/ neech chaakri bheek nidaar*, i.e., farming is the best, followed by trade, but service is lowly and begging is the lowliest (Chand 14). If a farmer wants bountiful crop, he is advised to sow barley and gram: *jo chahve kisaannaaj Ghana, tai bo de jau chanaa*. There is an interesting clash of ego between the grains—wheat and millet (*bajra*): *bajra kahai main bada albela/ do moosal tain ladun akela/ jo meri khichdi khave, fool faal kothi ho jaave*, i.e., millet says "I am a knight among grains, for I fight two cudgels single-handedly [reference to the thrashing process]; the one who eats food containing me becomes super strong." How would wheat lag behind, so it retorts: *Gehun kahe main bada gambheer, sab bahiyon mein hun ameer/ mere bin na poori pakvaan, aaye gaye ka raakhun maan*, i.e., "I am the richest among all grains, without me no food is complete or sumptuous. I am the one who accords deserved respect to the guests" (Punia in Bansal 112). To underline the importance of tilling the land, a *karka* is dedicated; *teri byahi daga desake, baahi dagi na de*, i.e., your wife might deceive you but not the tilling on land (Chand 26). There is fine linguistic parallelism in the words 'byahi' (marriage) and 'baahi' (tilling). Similarly, *jis khet men khasam na ja, va khet khasam ne kha*, i.e., the farm which your husband does not attend to, will eat him up (Chand 67). Here, one finds the humour-laden term 'khasam' for husband and nice end-rhyme.

The rigours of farming are hinted at in this *karka*: *Kheti hondi sehli, te kar lainde dhobi teli maati gailan hove maati, aathon pehar ki gola laathi*, i.e., If farming could be easy, then even the washermen and oil extractor could have done it. You have to be one with the soil and it is an arduous 24-hour task (Chand 49). Haryanvi *karka* proscribes lethargy in this profession: *aalas neend kisan ne khove, chor ne khove khansi/ taka byaj mool ne khove, raand ne khove haansi*, i.e., Laziness destroys farmer and coughing the thief/ even small interest rate wastes the capital loan amount and laughing destroys the widow (Mathana 58). Here, no doubt, the repressive treatment of widow is indicated which is a historical fact, although with changing times, attitude towards widows is changing.

As stated earlier, these verses or *karke* remind one of the ancient Greek poet Hesiod's *Works and Days*, in which he guides his lazy brother Perses about farming: "Hunger is altogether a meet comrade for the sluggard. Both gods and men are angry with a man who lives idle, for in nature he is like the stingless drones who waste the labour of the bees, eating without working; but let it be your care to order your work properly, that in the right season your barns may be full of victual" (293-319).

Farm animals like cows, oxen and buffalos are precious commodities for any agriculturalist in Haryana. The importance of cow is underlined here: *gehun bhojan, gau dhan, ghar sulakhni naar/ chauthi peeth turang ki, surag nisaani chaar*, i.e., food containing wheat, the wealth of cows, good natured housewife, a horse to ride—these are the four attributes of a heavenly home (Punia in Bansal 115). Regarding oxen, there is the *karka* laying down the thumb rule regarding value: *laakha le liyo laakh ka, leela le liyo karorh/ dhaula ne liyo vaah baah kai, par peela deeno chhod*, i.e., buy the brown ox for a lakh of rupees, the blue for a crore of rupees, but check the white one by plying it and leave the yellow one as worthless (*ibid.* 116).

It may be noted here that it is common to find contradictory opinions on things. Thus, cow may be venerated here, but buffalo seems a better option to some. So, there is the *karka* to this effect also: *Bakri bakri gaai janjaal, doodh peena tai bhains nu paal*, i.e., goat and cow are a bother, if you want to drink milk, then raise a buffalo (*ibid.* 116). The upkeep of animals is of paramount importance: *Byandi ar dhanandi tai door mat jaana/ gailan rehve jo dhani ne na pade pistana* (Chand 15), i.e., when the cow or buffalo has given birth to a young one or is ready to deliver, the owner [considered rich because he has cattle] must stay nearby lest he has to regret later.

But the Haryanvi mindset is equally concerned about the mental health of the animal. An old ox does not like to work but "retire," so to say. His mindset is revealed in a folk song: *Are nyun rove Buddha bail, mane mat beche re papi/ tera kuan-kolhu main chalya, naaj kamaa ke tere ghar ghaalya/ ib tain Karli bajar ki chhati*, i.e., The old ox weeps and says, "O sinful farmer, do not sell me [because] I worked on your farm wheel [all through] and filled your granary with grains. Now you have stiffened your heart [to sell me away because I am old]" (Kadyan in Bansal 79). It is not that only the route to prosperity or caution against poverty is in focus, the pauper has his own kind of joy: *gaai na baachhi; neend aave aachhi*, i.e., If you have neither cow, nor calf, you get sound sleep [for there is no worrying about theft] (Mathana 57).

The agriculture in Haryana has always been slave to rains. Forecasting rain with *karke* is easy: *aadhe kaatak gardfard na le thaman ka naam/ eebe chokas ho lio, saadh men, thada barse Ram*, i.e., When during the month of *Kartik*, thundering continues unabated, then be alert because during the month of *Asaadh*, it will rain heavily (Chand 70). There is an entire range of *karke* dealing with different months of the Indian *Vikrami* calendar. Some of them are produced here: *Chait chharpara to saanvan nirmala*, i.e., if it rains in *Chait*, it won't in *Saanvan* [the usual month of rain], and *Jeth chale purvai, saanvan dhool uthai*, i.e., if easterly wind blows in the month of *Jeth*, then the month of *Saanvan* will see only dust-storms (Mathana 52).

Hesiod too lays down: "When the Pleiades, daughters of Atlas, are rising, begin your harvest, and your ploughing when they are going to set. Forty nights and days they are hidden and appear again as the year moves round, when first you sharpen your sickle" (Hesiod 383-404). Again: "Mark, when you hear the voice of the crane [middle of November] who cries year by year from the clouds above, for she gives the signal for ploughing and shows the season of rainy winter" (Hesiod 448-57). Besides, "Set your slaves to winnow Demeter's holy grain, when strong Orion first appears" (Hesiod 597-608). Here, Hesiod is referring to the month of July.

Haryanvi *karke* also predict famine: *din men tai garmi sataave, raat oas kamaal/ jai bole kaag raat na, te bhatthu pade kaal*, i.e., When the days are hot but at night you get dew drops and the crow caws at night, then will come the worst famine for sure (Chand 72). Similarly, *do saaman do bhaadve, do kaatik do maah/ sona chandi bech kai naaj bisawan ja,* i.e., in a year with two months of Saawan, Bhaadon or Kaartik[3], it is better to invest all your money in storing grains [for there would be famine] (Chand 50).

There are tips for health too; moderation is the key*: khao peeo chhiko mat, chaalo firo, thakko mat; bolo chaalo bakko mat, dekho bhaalo takko mat*, i.e. eat and drink but do not binge, walk and roam about but don't get tired; talk but don't talk rot, look about everything but do not stare (Chand 57). Here is the indication of good health: *pet narm paanh garm, aur sir thanda; aave vaid, te besak dikhaay danda,* i.e., When your stomach is soft and feet warm and head cool, then don't be afraid of the doctor and if he visits your house, show him the stick! (Chand 83). Obviously, the lathi-wielding farmer of Haryana would love this reference!

In matters of worldly relationships, the ancient texts like Vedas seem to have inspired the Haryanvi *karke*, as for example, *anya sahajjano bhrata, shatru sahodarah* (Rig Veda 1/105/17), i.e., Other's relative is our brother, while our close relative is our enemy. This has some affinity with the *karka: ghar ka door padosi nede* or the intimate relation is stranger but the neighbour is closer to heart (Punia in Bansal 112). Hesiod's advice about monetary dealings with relatives has a note of caution too: "Let the wage promised to a friend be fixed; even with your brother smile—and get a witness; for trust and mistrust, alike ruin men" (370-72).

The highly respected elders in a Haryanvi family ought to be given due regard, as this *karka* prescribes: *jis ghar Buddha na maaniye, dhori pade na ghaas/ saas bahu ki ho ladai, ujad ho jaye baas*, i.e., The house where the elderly is not obeyed, nor do animals get fodder/ where there is always tiff between daughter-in-law and the mother-in-law, that house is bound to turn into desolation (Mharaharyana). There are wisecracks in the form of insightful observations on different communities like: *bhookha Brahmin soye, aur bhookha jaat roye; bhookha baaniya hanse, aur bhookha raaghad kamar kasse*, i.e., if a Brahmin is hungry, he will sleep and if a Jaat (the dominant community in Haryana) is hungry, he will cry; a hungry Baniya [trader by caste] will laugh [thinking he has saved money on food!], but a Raaghad [a feared martial caste] will get ready for action [to snatch from someone] (Sharma 134).

These *karke*, using simple language and rhyme are easy to remember. At the same time, they have some literary merit too, what with alliteration, pun and metaphors used in most of them. What these nuggets of rural folk wisdom prove is that truth is simple though multi-pronged. One can find sometimes contradictions as with regard to one's preference for cow or buffalo. On that count, however, there is no scope for conflict. Secondly, these *karke* or verses contain local truths as also universal ones. There are verses laying down local attitude towards, say women, but there are also comments on human nature which are universally valid like laziness is antagonistic to prosperity. The comparison with the Vedas and the Greek poet raises their worth above temporal and territorial limitations. While the simple folks can put up with differences, the problem of the intellectual class the world over is to yearn for a generalized statement that befits all beings, conditions, situations, and so on. But as G.B. Shaw noted: "The golden rule is that there are no golden rules" (261).

This yearning for a cover-all truth is the point of departure in all ideologies and theoretical frameworks which clash with each other claiming to be the sole preserve of truth. The unaccommodative layers of civilizational perceptions, social procedures and epistemological tools have rendered truth complex and discussions acrimonious, whereas truth can be seen somewhat like the way the narrator in William Saroyan's story "The Pomegranate Trees" describes the desert: "It was a region of loneliness, emptiness, truth and dignity. It was the nature at its proudest, driest, loneliest and loveliest." The Haryanvi *karke* or verses contain truth in its bare or naked form.

NOTES

1. The term "Haryanvi" is the Hindi adjective of Haryana and means "belonging to Haryana." Haryana is a prosperous state of India surrounding Delhi, the national capital of India on three sides.
2. All citations are in Haryanvi dialect (my translation). The principle of equivalence has been subordinated to that of domestication, so that the reader of English translation can comprehend the meaning. For that purpose, some "gloss" in the form of elaboration has been added.
3. Indian calendar (Vikrami Samvat) is based on the lunar cycle. In order to adjust for the mismatch between twelve lunar cycles (354 lunar days) and nearly 365 solar days, it inserts an extra full month, every four years.

Works Cited

Bansal, Kumud. *Haryana ka Lok Sahitya*. Panchkula: Haryana Sahitya Akademi, 2017.

Chand, Sumer. *Mahri Dadi Nani Wali Kahni*. Delhi: Mehak, 2009.

___. *Mahre Karke Kisse*. Delhi: Mehak, 2010.

Deswal, Santram. "Haryana ke Lok Sahitya ki Anamit Vidhayen," in Kumud Bansal, pp. 41-52.

Hesiod. *Works and Days*, trans. Hugh Evelyn White, 1914.

http://www.sacred-texts.com/cla/hesiod/works.htm.

Kadyan, Om Prakash. "Haryana ke lok geeton ka sanskritik Adhyayan," in Kumud Bansal, pp. 53-81.

Mathana, Raghubir Singh. *Hariyana: Kahavton ke Jharokhe Me*. Kaithal: Sukirti, 2011.

Mharaharyana. http://www.mharaharyana.com/article-details/202/ haryanvi-proverbs.html

Punia, Maha Singh. "Hariyanvi lokoktiyon men rachi basi kisaani sanskriti," in Kumud Bansal, pp. 107-18.

Saroyan, William: "The Pomegranate Trees." *My Name is Aram*. Berne-Paris: Phoenix, 1947, pp. 145-58.

Sharma, Jai Prakash. *Hariyanvi Lok Sahitya ka Samaajik Adhyayan*. Panchkula: Haryana Sahitya Akademi, 2008.

Shaw, G.B. "Maxims for Revolutionists," *Man and Superman*. Middleton, UK: Penguin, 1903, Rpt. 1977.